Charles Dickens

IMMORTALS OF LITERATURE

CHARLES DICKENS

by Charles Haines

Franklin Watts, Inc.
575 Lexington Avenue
New York, N.Y. 10022

for The Persi Generation

All photographs, including
cover, courtesy
Charles Phelps Cushing

Contents

T 1511803

Introduction

If to be famous is to be great, Charles Dickens is one of the greatest writers that ever lived. Today, some one hundred years after his death, his novels are reprinted, read, and remembered more than those of any other English novelist. They have been translated into more than fifty languages. They have been filmed and adapted for the stage and transformed into musical comedy. Dickens is still the best-known and most popular English novelist of them all.

One can like Dickens's novels, or one can dislike them. One can admire them, or one can say that they are not good. But one cannot ignore them.

In the first place, Dickens created—he did not just talk about or describe—people and places. Mr. Micawber and Mr. Pecksniff and Aunt Betsey Trotwood. Sydney Carton and Sam Weller and Mrs. Gamp. Mr. Pickwick and Mr. Chadband and Major Bagstock. Some of his characters are funny, some of them are ludicrous, some are dramatic. It is true that most of them have not the depth of a Shakespearean character, nor are they seen from as many points of view as a Tolstoyan character. What of that? They are brilliant players of parts on the stage of the Dickens World. They may be no more "true" than the lady "sawed in half" by a magician during his performance, but they amuse us, many of them; they fascinate us, they entertain us. "All the world's a stage, and all the men and women merely players." Shakespeare, in spite of those words in *As You Like It*, created more than "merely players." It is Dickens that created the players. They talk and laugh and strut and fret. We shut the book. The lights in the theater come up. They are gone. But they were there. We know they were there. They still exist somewhere.

In the second place, Dickens makes us laugh. His novels are about a human comedy that is very often funny. It is not easy to laugh much harder than when we read about Mr. Micawber or about Jingle or about Mrs. Gamp. Sometimes Dickens is bitter, and we laugh. Sometimes his characters are ridiculous, and we laugh. Sometimes we laugh because Dickens is so eccentric and so tender at once.

In the third place, Dickens (like Shelley) had a "passion for reforming the world." He attacked public wrongdoing and private sin. He wrote about the wretched lives led by the poor. He laughed at the pompousness of snobs and social climbers. He wrote often and with great compassion of the miserable existences of orphans and workhouse children. He cheered virtue wherever he found it.

In all of his writings, Dickens's heart was in the right place. That is a great deal.

Dickens at his best was a creator, a humorist, and a reformer. At times, he could also be (it must be admitted) long-winded and embarrassingly sentimental. There are not many people today who enjoy reading about Little Nell in *The Old Curiosity Shop* or who are not bored by Esther Summerson and Lucie Manette. Sometimes (it seems) Dickens's creative, humorous, and reforming powers failed him all at the same time. What he wrote at those times we yawn as we read. But we go on reading. (Even when Dickens is not at his best, he is rarely downright dull.) After a few pages or a few chapters, or sometimes after nearly a whole book, we find that we are back in the best part of the Dickens World. All is well again.

It is not surprising that the person that wrote these startling and vivid novels was a startling and vivid man. It is hardly surprising to find out that he was himself a true Dickensian character. Dickens was a young man in a hurry, and a middle-aged man in a rush. He was at one minute extremely warmhearted and generous, and the next minute cold and distant. He had a robust, infectious sense of humor; and he had a stern sense of business that made him drive hard financial bargains, sometimes at the expense of friendships. For most of his life he actively sought popularity, the applause—the adoration—of the public. It was, in fact, his constant search for the limelight and the handclapping that killed him before his time. Yet, in his will, he stipulated that he be buried in "an inexpensive, unostentatious, and strictly private manner."

Dickens's novels are all, to a large extent, parts of the story of his life. Most of the places that he describes in them are places that he knew. Many of his great characters are highly-colored portraits of his family, his friends, and acquaintances. He himself appears repeatedly, a part here and a part there, in various guises in the course of his writings. One of his best novels, *David Copperfield*, is quite plainly his autobiography. It was his own favorite among the books that he wrote.

A great deal is known about the life of Dickens. His friend John Forster wrote a biography of him. (Another friend, Wilkie Collins, called Forster's biography—not altogether inaccurately—"The Life of John Forster, with occasional anecdotes of Charles Dickens.") A modern scholar, Edgar Johnson, has written an exhaustive and admirably readable life of Dickens. There are biographies, too, by Hesketh Pearson, Jack Lindsay, and Una Pope-Hennessy. Books on Dickens by Charles Wagenknecht, George Ford, Steven Marcus, Humphrey House, and K. J. Fielding make full use of letters, book reviews, and diaries of the Victorian Age. I have turned to the works by these writers, and by others, in writing the pages that follow.

I have not tried to tell the "whole story," that is, to put down all the known facts of Dickens's life. Enough is, at some times and in some places, too much. I have tried, instead, to give an idea of what sort of man Dickens was. What sort of man and what sort of writer was it, of whom Longfellow could say, when he heard that Dickens had died, "I never knew an author's death to cause such general mourning." Or of whom Mary Cowden Clarke, the

Shakespeare scholar, said at the same time, "The sun seemed suddenly blotted out." And Thomas Carlyle, "It is an event world wide. His death has 'eclipsed [we, too, may say] the harmless gaiety of nations.' "

Mrs. D. K. Wood not only typed and retyped the manuscript of this book, but she also read, while I was writing, many works by Dickens and about Dickens in order to be in a position to make many useful suggestions. I owe her a great debt of gratitude.

CHARLES HAINES

Charles Dickens

CHAPTER 1

Childhood

Charles Dickens was born on February 7, 1812, at Land-port, near the city of Portsmouth, England. His father, John, was a clerk in a Navy Pay Office. John Dickens was a friendly, good-natured, well-read man, as well as a loving husband and a devoted parent. He had, however, one fault that nearly offset all his virtues: he had absolutely no sense of money. It was not that he gambled his income away or spent too much of it in taverns. He simply let it slip through his fingers. He would invite friends to his house for dinners that he could not afford. He would give his wife and children expensive presents that were soon broken or lost. Although he worked hard and was paid well enough, because he was such a spendthrift, his family lived constantly on the brink of poverty, and more than once they were tumbled into misery and destitution.

All might have been well if Charles Dickens's mother had had the financial sense that her husband lacked; but she had not. In fact, she was as easygoing and as careless about money as he was. It has often been pointed out that

Mr. Micawber, in *David Copperfield,* and Mrs. Nickleby, in *Nicholas Nickleby*, are Dickens's sketches of his mother and father. They were good-hearted, loving parents, but they were also improvident and, in a way, silly people. They had eight children altogether (two of whom died in infancy), and they were unable to provide decently for any of them.

Charles Dickens was a bright, active child. He was small for his age, but he was full of imagination and high spirits. His mother taught him to read, and she taught him a little Latin while he was very young. Soon he was devouring all the books he could lay his hands on. He would sit by the hour reading *Robinson Crusoe* or *Don Quixote* or *Tom Jones.* He early showed that he had another talent. He could sing funny songs to a group of his father's dinner guests, without a trace of shyness, and he could recite poems and snatches from plays for them.

Clerks in Navy Pay Offices were transferred from place to place frequently, and at short notice. The Dickenses lived for a few years in London. Then they moved to Chatham, a small city about thirty-five miles east of London, and then back to London again. Since John Dickens never learned financial responsibility, the family members were constantly forced to think up schemes to increase their income. One of their first schemes was to take in boarders. Charles's aunt had been left a widow, and then had married a Dr. Matthew Lamert. Dr. Lamert had a son, James, by his first marriage. James Lamert boarded with the Dickenses for several years. He was a pleasant young man, who often took young Charles on outings around

London and to the theater. But the money that he paid for his room and board did not even begin to solve the Dickens family's perennial financial problem.

Charles Dickens went to school for a while at Giles Academy in Chatham, where Mr. Giles, the headmaster, encouraged him to go on with his reading. In 1822 John Dickens was transferred back to London again, and in the spring of 1823 Charles had to leave Giles Academy and go to London, too. When he left Chatham for London that year, young Charles entered on the darkest period of his childhood.

John Dickens had taken a house for the family in a part of London known as Camden Town. Charles was now eleven, and he could easily see that this Camden Town house was a poor one in a squalid part of the city. He was more distressed when he found out that his parents planned not to send him to school anymore: they could not afford to. Instead, he was expected to help with the housework and to run errands. This was a great disappointment to the boy who had recently received so much pleasure from reading, writing, and studying.

Things got worse. In a desperate effort to make some money, Mrs. Dickens decided to open a school for girls. That September, she spent a badly needed £50 on the rental of a house in Gower Street in London. She had a big brass plaque hammered onto the front door. It read, "Mrs. Dickens's Establishment." She also had some advertising circulars printed. Young Charles wandered up one street and down the next, leaving a circular at every house. But not one single student ever presented herself at "Mrs. Dickens's Establishment."

The pawnshop was the family's next hope. Again, Charles was sent out on errands, this time to sell chairs, tables, and all but the most essential furniture. Even John Dickens's books were sold. With tears in his eyes, Charles took *Tom Jones* and *Robinson Crusoe* and the others down to a bookstore in Hampstead Road and sold them. Not only did these measures fail to bring in enough money for the family to be comfortable, but John Dickens was coming closer and closer every day to being arrested and imprisoned for debt.

Then the blow fell. James Lamert now had a job as the manager of a small factory. The plant produced "blacking," the thick, dark paste that people used to spread onto their wood- and coal-burning stoves in order to protect the metal. Lamert suggested to the Dickenses that Charles be put to work in the blacking factory—which had the evil-sounding address of "30 Hungerford Stairs, the Strand." John Dickens and his wife were now nearly desperate for money. James Lamert was making the suggestion with the best of good intentions. His idea was accepted. Two days after his twelfth birthday, young Charles trudged across London at 7:30 in the morning, and took up his duties as potboy in Warren's Blacking Factory.

Many boys of twelve had jobs in England in the early 1800's, and many of the jobs they held involved much harder and much dirtier work than Charles's labors among the blacking pots. Boys of six, seven, and eight spent ten and twelve hours a day going up and down the insides of chimneys, cleaning out soot and birds' nests. Others, not much older, spent all their waking hours as crossing sweepers. They would stand at busy corners of London streets, with heavy brooms in their hands, sweeping away the mud, garbage, and horse manure that had collected. There were very few child labor laws in the world at that time, and children were looked on by many people as simply so many more mouths to feed.

So it was that Charles Dickens, too, became a working boy. In fairness to his parents and to James Lamert, it must be noted that his job was not a difficult one. He was to work from 8:00 in the morning until 8:00 at night, with an hour off for lunch and half an hour off for tea. His task at the factory was to paste labels on the pots of blacking. He was to be paid six shillings a week (about $6.00 today), which was considered a high wage for a boy in those days. Lamert also offered to give him some school lessons during his lunch hour.

But the factory itself was an old, leaky, tumbledown building. Rats swarmed through it. The air was fetid and stank horribly. Young Charles soon became adept at pasting on the labels, but he was brokenhearted. The wound made by his blacking factory days never entirely healed. It is true that his work there was not physically painful or mentally crippling. It is true that he spent only about four months altogether at the job. But suddenly, at the age of twelve, he was forced to grow up in an instant. He saw how wretched life could be. He saw that many children were condemned, from the time they were hardly more than babies until the day they died, to a life of endless drudgery. He saw what *might have been* his lot and what *was*, in fact, the lot of thousands. And he never forgot.

Things seemed bad enough to young Charles in the early part of February, 1824, but worse was yet to come. On February 20, his father was arrested for debt. He owed £40 to a man named James Karr. All his worldly assets amounted to £10. According to the law of the time, a man who was unable to pay his debts was sent to jail. So, on February 23, the gates of Marshalsea Prison swung shut behind Charles Dickens's father.

The future for the Dickens family looked very dark indeed. John Dickens was still officially employed by the Navy Pay Office. If he had himself declared bankrupt (in order to wipe out his debts and be released from prison), the Navy Pay Office would have fired him. If he were fired, he would lose his pension. If he did not declare bankruptcy, he would be kept in prison. Finally, he hit upon the scheme of having himself declared physically unable to continue as a Navy Pay Office clerk. He hoped by this means to be retired and to be given his pension. But before his case was considered, an unexpected happening set him free. On April 24, 1824, John Dickens's mother died. In her will, she left her impecunious son £450. The debt to James Karr was paid. John Dickens left Marshalsea Prison, a free man again.

By June of that year, young Charles had been taken out of the blacking factory and sent to the Wellington House Academy. He did well at the school. He won several prizes, in spite of the fact that he spent a great deal of his time training white mice to climb ladders and to pull tiny carts.

Charles turned out to be a healthy, good-looking, smart, popular student. His father finally got his release and his pension from the Navy Pay Office and took a job as a parliamentary reporter for a newspaper. The saddest days of Charles Dickens's early life were over.

CHAPTER 2

Love

Charles Dickens left Wellington House Academy early in the spring of 1827. He was just fifteen years old. In May, he became a clerk and messenger boy in a lawyer's office in London. During his spare time, he taught himself shorthand. It took him eighteen months to master the system. The minute that he felt sure of his ability, he quit his job and set himself up as a free-lance shorthand reporter in the court known as Doctors' Commons.

Doctors' Commons (it no longer exists today) was the nineteenth-century London court that dealt with such things as wills and divorces. It was Dickens's job, and the job of the other free-lance court reporters, to go to the Doctors' Commons buildings every day and wait for some lawyer to ask him to come into the courtroom and take down every word that was said. Then he was to go into another room and transcribe his shorthand into longhand. It was dull work, but Dickens did it well. He quickly earned the reputation of being the best reporter in the court. He also formed, at the same time, a markedly unfavorable impression of judges and lawyers in general. He found them dull, dishonest, and endlessly talkative.

For his eighteenth birthday, Dickens gave himself an important present: it was a pass to the reading room of the British Museum library. From then on, for some time, every minute that he was not taking down shorthand reports at Doctors' Commons, he spent doing one of two things. He either read or he memorized parts in plays. As a result of his life as a court reporter, he had decided that he wanted to become an actor.

Something happened in 1830, however, that was to change Dickens's entire life. He met Maria Beadnell.

Miss Beadnell was the daughter of a bank manager named George Beadnell. There were three beautiful Beadnell daughters: Margaret, Anne, and Maria, the youngest. Maria was a year older than Charles. She had bright eyes, black hair, and a ravishing smile. She was an angel. Or such, at least, Dickens believed her to be from the very instant he set eyes on her. Maria could play the harp, and Dickens was sure that if only Satan could have heard her, he would have regretted his revolt in heaven, and would have reformed and returned to paradise.

Dickens loved Maria Beadnell with all the intensity and all the devotion of his passionate, energetic nature. He went to her house as often as he could. He wrote poems for her. He wrote letters to her. He ran errands for her all over London. Once she gave him a pair of blue gloves to match something for her. He was in ecstasy. When he was alone, he held imaginary conversations with her; and he rehearsed the speech that he would make to her mother, asking permission to marry Maria: "Honoured Madam, I think that a lady gifted with those powers of observation which I know you to possess . . . can scarcely have failed to discover that I love your adorable daughter deeply, devotedly. . . ."

Charles worked harder and faster still at Doctors' Commons. In his imagination, he spent all the money that he was going to earn on a house and furniture and clothes for Mrs. Maria Dickens. Maria had penetrated every corner and chink and crevice of his being. He was ecstatically in love.

He was also in agony. The Beadnells did not look kindly on young Charles Dickens as a future son-in-law. Mr. Beadnell did not ever even learn to pronounce his name correctly. To the rather haughty bank manager, the young man was always "Mr. Dickin." Fathers have a way of not estimating depth of devotion—where their daughters are concerned—as highly as promising careers. And mothers have a way of going along with fathers. Dickens was only a court reporter. He would never be able to keep Maria "in the style to which she had been accustomed." He was a witty and pleasant boy, but, after all, his father had been in prison. Dickens was hurt but not discouraged. He asked Henry Kolle, who was engaged to Anne Beadnell, to speak up in his favor. He was offered advice and sympathy by one of Maria's friends, a girl named Marianne Leigh. At least once every day, sometimes late at night when everyone was in bed, Charles would walk past Maria's house and silently swear eternal devotion outside her darkened window.

These measures might have done some good if Maria had loved Charles. But she did not. She was amused by him. She was flattered by his dauntless ardor. She laughed at his jokes and applauded prettily when he sang a song. But that was all. Maria was a flirt. She played with his affections, and perhaps she laughed secretly at his agony. It took Dickens nearly three years to realize that Maria would never love him, that she would probably never love anybody, that she would not become Mrs. Dickens, that they would not spend their lives together in the permanent bliss of mutual adoration. Finally, too, Maria's parents intervened. They forbade Dickens to come to their house anymore, and they sent Maria off to school in Paris.

Gradually reason penetrated the fog of Dickens's adoration. He saw what a tease and flirt Maria was and had always been. He sent back the letters that she had written to him—all tied up with a piece of ribbon the very shade of blue of the gloves that he had been sent to match for her. In May, 1833, he wrote her one final letter. It was more calm and balanced in tone than a letter one might have expected from a twenty-one-year-old boy whose affections had been led on and played with by a flirtatious little minx: "I have never loved and I can never love any human creature breathing but yourself. We have had many differences and we have lately been entirely separated. Absence, however, has not altered my feelings in the slightest degree, and the love that I now tender you is as pure and as lasting as at any period of our former correspondence . . . The matter, now, of course, rests solely with you . . ."

13

The answer that Maria made to this last outburst of passion and sincerity was superficial and quarrelsome. All was over.

At first, the story of Dickens's love for Maria Beadnell sounds very like the story of many infatuations. There are many Maria Beadnells in this world, and most men have sighed outside the window of at least one of them. Men rarely marry their Maria Beadnells; whether they ever forget them or not is another matter. Dickens certainly never forgot his.

There are several sequels to the story of Charles Dickens's first love. It seems to be part of the nature of a young man when he is rejected by the girl that he loves to think to himself, "I'll show her! I'll became famous and important. Then she'll be sorry! Then she'll come to me and plead. She'll beg that I take her back! And I. . . ." Here the dreams vary. Some young men dream that they will take her back. Some dream that, stern and inflexible, they will say coldly, "No! Now it is your turn to suffer, as then you made me suffer!" Dickens was to know every one of the possible joys that can be given the rejected suitor.

Of course, Dickens did become famous. Within only three years of the date of his final letter to Maria, he had become one of the best-known men in England. His *Pickwick Papers* was the delight of the world. Surely Maria Beadnell, pouting in her corner of the kingdom, must have known this and must have stamped her pretty little foot over and over again in anger and disappointment. If only she had known that her adoring little court reporter would so soon become the most famous writer in the world! But she did not know it. The Marias never do.

She married a prosperous businessman named Henry Louis Winter. She became the mother of two girls. The girls began to grow up. Finally, she could contain herself no longer. In February, 1855, she wrote Dickens a letter. After twenty-two years, Dickens instantly recognized her handwriting on the envelope. He read her lines. He was, not surprisingly, overjoyed to hear from her—overjoyed sincerely, not vindictively. They exchanged several letters. In an instant Dickens had been seized once more by the old feeling of adoration. Maria and he decided to meet. They set the date for February 25. Dickens was then forty-three years old, a handsome, trim, vigorous man. When he saw Maria Beadnell Winter he was—for the second time, but now for very different reasons—heartbreakingly disappointed.

Maria had grown into a foolish, affected, unlovely woman. Her girlish laugh had become a nervous giggle. Her stream of magic conversation had become empty, high-pitched chatter. Although she was in her forties, she continued to try to act like the enchanting girl that she once had been. One of the most depressing sights in the world is that of a woman of forty who does not realize that she is no longer a girl of twenty.

Dickens and Maria met a second time, a few days later, and she twittered and giggled and chirped some more. She had a cold, too, and Dickens caught it. Maria suggested that they meet again—and again. But by this time Dickens had really had enough. He told her that he was busy, that he was going away, that he did not feel well. By a strange turn of fate, now it was Dickens that rejected Maria. At last Maria understood. She wrote him no more letters. She implored him no further. They had come to the end of their road.

Even so, Maria Beadnell is immortal. Not as Maria Beadnell, but as Dora, David Copperfield's child-wife. Very few people have read Dickens's descriptions of Dora without being touched to the heart—or have failed to recognize that the writer of those lines had, in his time, adored the woman of whom he was writing, and his heart had been broken by her:

"Will you call me a name I want you to call me?" inquired Dora, without moving.

"What is it?" I asked with a smile.

"It's a stupid name," she said, shaking her curls for a moment. "Child-wife."

I laughingly asked my child-wife what her fancy was in desiring to be so called. She answered without moving, otherwise than as the arm I twined about her may have brought her blue eyes nearer to me:

"I don't mean, you silly fellow, that you should use the name instead of Dora. I only mean that you should think of me that way. When you are going to be angry with me, say to yourself, 'it's only my child-wife!' When I am very disappointing, say, 'I knew, a long time ago, that she would make but a child-wife!' When you miss what I should like to be, and I think can never be, say, 'still my foolish child-wife loves me!' For indeed I do."

CHAPTER 3

The Incredible Young Man

Early in 1832, Dickens had given up his work at Doctors' Commons and had taken a job as a reporter. Actually, he had taken two jobs. One was with a newspaper called the *True Sun*. The other was with the *Mirror of Parliament*, a journal that printed and published all the things that were said by the country's lawmakers in the House of Commons and in the House of Lords.

The 1830's were ten very important years in the history of England. It was during those years that England changed from an agricultural country into an industrial nation. Historians have termed this change the Industrial Revolution. Until the 1830's, England had been a nation of farmers. After the 1830's, England became a nation of manufacturers. The main factor in this shift from agriculture to industry was the invention and the development of the steam engine. Steam engines were first put to work principally as railroad locomotives, and railroads changed the face of England and of the world.

The historical importance of the building of the railroads

cannot be overemphasized. In 1820, a man might have spent four days traveling from, say, London to Liverpool. The journey was uncomfortable, unsafe, and expensive. In 1840, after the railroads had been built, that same journey took less than one day, and was cheap, safe, and relatively comfortable. So, people began to travel. They left the land and moved to the cities. Food and manufactured goods were distributed around the country more easily. News traveled faster. What happened in London in the morning could be printed in a newspaper and read about in Manchester in the evening. Postal services were organized. As letters and up-to-date newspapers and books became more generally available, more and more people wanted to study and to learn to read. Numbers of new schools and universities were founded.

As the people began to move from the country to the cities, new problems arose. There was the question of pure water, sanitation, and sewage. Public health regulations had to be set up. There was the question of law and order. Police forces modeled after London's "Bobbies" (organized by, and named after, Sir Robert Peel) were soon at work in every city in England. New laws and regulations governing fire prevention and housing and city transportation had to be made. Naturally, the question arose as to who was to make these laws. In the year 1832, the first Reform Bill was passed. It was the first step in the process that transferred voting rights and legislative authority from the hands of the rich and aristocratic few into the hands of all the people.

The now famous names of many men were closely connected with all these processes of change. There was Thomas Babington Macaulay, later Lord Macaulay, who did much to insure the passage of the Reform Bill of 1832 and much to see that humane child labor laws were set up. There was William Wilberforce, who worked to bring about the abolition of slavery in the British Empire. There was Lord John Russell, who twice became Prime Minister of England. There was Daniel O'Connell, who agitated vigorously for Irish independence. There was the Duke of Wellington (the "Iron Duke") and William Gladstone, just beginning a political career that was to last for more than sixty years.

From his uncomfortable reporter's perch high in the gallery of the Parliament buildings, Dickens heard all these men, and more, debate and argue and question. When he was on duty, he did not miss a syllable of what was said. "There never was such a shorthand reporter!" one of his colleagues said of him admiringly. Few men in the country knew better than the twenty-one-year-old Charles Dickens what was going on in England.

Dickens did not like very much of what he saw. Some attention, he felt, was being given to the plight of the poor and the orphans, the old, the sick, and the prisoners, but not enough. Some laws were being passed to keep the cities and the factories safe and clean, but they were not being passed fast enough. Dickens saw that there was a strange, distressing similarity of character between almost all of England's lawmakers and little Maria Beadnell. They talked a great deal, but they did not say very much. They smiled and made promises, but they broke their promises.

Clearly, they did not feel in their hearts the agony and the distress of thousands of the people whom it was their job to govern. Like Maria Beadnell, the lawmakers were fickle and false. They may have had brains; they were sadly lacking in heart.

Dickens decided that something must be done to wake up the country, and he would try to do it. He would become, if he could, the conscience of the land. He had failed in his love for Maria Beadnell. He knew what it was to be a factory drudge. Now he was going to come to the aid of hundreds of thousands of Englishmen who were suffering, too, for an endless variety of reasons. But he was not going to do it by becoming a lawyer or a judge or a member of Parliament. The real cure for both social and personal sadness, Dickens felt, lay less in wise laws and reform movements than it did in charity and compassion within each single heart, and in "little, nameless, unremembered acts of kindness and of love."

The decision to speak out on behalf of the lowly, the miserable, the sick, and the forgotten was not a decision that Dickens made consciously. Rather, because he himself had had his love rejected and had been badly dealt with by his parents, he could feel sympathy spontaneously for others. To protect himself against being hurt any more, he unconsciously determined to put his deepest emotions into fiction, rather than into his everyday life. In many of the things that he did in the course of his life, Dickens the man was often cold or self-centered or stern, but in all of the books that he wrote, Dickens the writer, with all his heart, sided with the downtrodden.

One evening late in 1833, Dickens walked down Fleet Street in London, turned off into a narrow, dark, side street called Johnson's Court, found the door to the offices of a publication named *Monthly Magazine*, and put into its mailbox the manuscript of a short sketch that he had written. Then, on an evening in December he went into a bookstore on the Strand and bought a copy of the *Monthly Magazine*. He opened it, turned its pages nervously, but (he hoped) casually. He was experiencing the feelings of every new writer who has sent a manuscript to a publisher. Had his work been accepted? Or would he later receive a formal and impersonal note?—"The editorial board has considered carefully . . . would like to thank you . . . feel that they cannot at this time use . . ." The sketch was there! *A Dinner at Poplar Walk.* It was not signed. The *Monthly Magazine*, a small publication, did not pay its contributors. But the piece had been published!

The editor of the magazine, a man named Holland, later sent Dickens a note to suggest that he write more "papers" and submit them. Dickens did. They were all accepted. In August, 1834, he signed one of his sketches for the first time. He used a pen name—Boz. He pronounced it to rhyme with "nose." In that same month, he was given a job as a parliamentary reporter with the *Morning Chronicle*, one of London's major newspapers.

Dickens's—Boz's—sketches were good. They were light; they were funny; they were warm. Boz began to acquire a modest fame. Harrison Ainsworth, one of the popular novelists of the day, wanted to make his acquaintance. The publisher John Macrone began to think of collecting the sketches and bringing them out in book form. When the managers of the *Morning Chronicle* decided to publish an evening edition, they agreed with George Hogarth, the editor of the new *Evening Chronicle*, that Dickens ought to be asked to contribute several Boz sketches to it. Dickens did. He was also invited several times to George Hogarth's house. Hogarth had a daughter named Catherine, who was just three years younger than Dickens. She had clear blue eyes and dark wavy hair that flowed down over her shoulders. Soon Dickens was paying daily visits to the Hogarth house.

Two years after *A Dinner at Poplar Walk* had been published, a young man named William Hall called on Dickens at his house. Hall was the junior partner in the new publishing firm of Chapman & Hall. He told Dickens that Chapman & Hall had recently decided to publish a series of drawings and cartoons by Robert Seymour, a well-known comic artist of the day. The drawings were going to be about an imaginary group of city men, who go into the country to hunt and fish and swim and skate. Would Dickens write a few lines of text by way of caption to go with each of Seymour's drawings? Dickens would. He would, he said, write the text to go with the drawings, but he would not write only a few lines. He would write twelve thousand words for each drawing. As he talked with Hall, he turned the original plan entirely around. The text would not accompany the drawings. The drawings would serve as illustrations of his text.

As Hall listened to the bright-eyed and determined twenty-three-year-old Boz, he must have had difficulty believing what he heard. Seymour was, after all, a well-known artist. Dickens was still only a minor writer. Before approaching Dickens, Hall had asked several famous men, including Theodore Hook and Leigh Hunt, to write the captions. They had all been too busy. Hall had come to Dickens as a nearly last resort. It ought to have flattered Dickens that he was being asked to work with a man as famous as Robert Seymour. But if Dickens was flattered, he gave little evidence of it. Hall was much impressed by Dickens, and by his proposal. He hurried away and per-suaded his partner, Edward Chapman, to accept the new idea; then Chapman and Hall together persuaded Seymour to go along with the plan. A contract was drawn up. Ac-cording to it, Dickens was to make his writing amusing and entertaining. Dickens set to work. He sat down at his desk, put some blank sheets of paper in front of him, and picked up a pen. And then, Dickens later said, "I thought of Mr. Pickwick."

The vigor of his imagination was astounding. He created the Pickwick Club. There was Mr. Pickwick himself, the roundest, kindest, most unworldly of men. There was Mr. Winkle, a would-be sportsman terrified of horses. There were Mr. Tupman, who wrongly believed himself a ladies' man, and Mr. Snodgrass, who thought that he could write poetry. Other characters swarmed in—Jingle, who could speak only in short nonsentences,

"Heads, heads—take care of your heads!" cried the loquacious stranger, as they came out under the low archway, which in those days formed the entrance to the coach-yard. "Terrible place—dangerous work—other day—five children—mother—tall lady, eating sandwiches—forgot the arch—crash—knock—children look round—mother's head off—sandwich in her hand—no mouth to put it in—head of a family off—shocking, shocking!"

and Sam Weller, who becomes Mr. Pickwick's valet, and Sam Weller's father. There is the fat boy, most unsubtle of lovers:

> The fat boy . . . applied himself assiduously to the pie.
> "What a nice young lady Miss Emily is!" said Mary, after a long silence.
> The fat boy had by this time finished the pie. He fixed his eyes on Mary, and replied—
> "I knows a nicerer."
> "Indeed!" said Mary.
> "Yes, indeed!" replied the fat boy, with unwonted vivacity.
> "What's her name?" inquired Mary.
> "What's yours?"
> "Mary."
> "So's hers," said the fat boy. "You're her." The boy grinned to add point to the compliment . . .

Dickens's powers of creation seemed inexhaustible. Only the first chapter of the book now known as *Pickwick Papers* does not sparkle. Of the other fifty-six chapters, it can be said that nothing as lively, as funny, or as amiable had been written in English since *Tristram Shandy*, and perhaps since Shakespeare had created Sir John Falstaff.

On March 31, 1836, the first installment of *Pickwick Papers* went on sale. And on April 2, Dickens and Catherine Hogarth were married at St. Luke's Church, Chelsea.

For reasons now not easy to understand, the first installment of *Pickwick* was not a success. One reviewer called it "excessively dull," and spoke of "exhausted comicality." The public bought few copies. Something had to be done. A meeting was arranged between Dickens and Robert Seymour. Seymour, not surprisingly, was angry and he blamed Dickens for the failure of the work. Dickens was unshaken by his anger, and as sure of himself as he had been on the day of his first interview with Hall. He refused any suggestion to change the plan for *Pickwick*. Seymour left him, still angry and very upset.

What happened next was sad and unexpected. No one knows exactly why he did it, but three days after his talk with Dickens, Robert Seymour went into a little summerhouse in his garden, put the muzzle of a rifle into his mouth, and blew out his brains.

Some men, on hearing of such a suicide, would have given up *Pickwick* forever. Dickens hardly paused in his work. He met with Chapman and Hall again. He convinced them that in spite of the bad reviews, in spite of the slender sales and the death of Seymour, they must not tamper with the formula of twelve thousand words of his text and a few drawings now to be done by some other artist. He persuaded the two men that the choice of the new artist ought to be left to him. He persuaded them, as well, to increase substantially the amount that they were to pay him. Dickens's self-confidence must have been astounding.

It is no less astounding to discover that his self-confidence proved to be entirely justified. Dickens wrote on, undaunted. As the *Pickwick* illustrator, he selected Hablôt Browne, a man two years younger than himself, who signed his work with the pseudonym "Phiz." In Chapter 10, Dickens created Sam Weller, and Sam Weller seized the public imagination. *Pickwick Papers* suddenly became the rage of England.

Four hundred copies of the first number of *Pickwick* had been printed. Forty thousand copies were sold of the installments that Dickens wrote after Chapter 10. Reviewers changed their minds entirely and said that Dickens was one of the greatest authors in the history of the country. Judges read *Pickwick* on the bench between cases (and perhaps during a few, as well). Cooks held the pages of *Pickwick* with one hand and stirred the soup with the other. Dickens had the faculty of being able to write in a way that delighted both young and old, the educated and the uneducated. People that could not read at all found someone to read *Pickwick* to them out loud. Children named their dogs and cats after *Pickwick* characters, and maiden ladies named their canary birds after them. Dickens had become, by July, 1836, one of the most famous men in England.

The fame, the clamor, and the adoration that went with *Pickwick* were no more than its due. *Pickwick* is a magic book, and a marvelously funny one. It does not have a plot or even a logical and regular plan. It simply took shape, as

Dickens wrote it, "like a genie from a bottle." The characters are, perhaps, "stock" characters, from the Don Quixote-like Mr. Pickwick to Sam Weller, his clever and irrepressible servant. In any hands but Dickens's, the book might have been dreary and only superficially clever. As Dickens wrote it, it has an atmosphere of fun and laughter that make it impossible for most people to put down. A nineteenth-century writer named Edmund Gosse described quite exactly the effect that *Pickwick* had on him, and has had on many readers since: "I felt myself to be in the company of a gentleman [Dickens] so extremely funny that I began to laugh before he began to speak; no sooner did he remark 'the sky was dark and gloomy, the air was damp and raw,' than I was in fits of laughter."

Few books have been written that are funnier than *Pickwick*. At the same time, there are few books that are sadder. One does not notice the sadness until one has read it three or four times, and even when one has noticed the sadness, one cannot stop laughing. The tears and the laughter are not pasted one on top of the other, but they are thoroughly and inextricably blended. *Pickwick* is a book about the human comedy. As such, it describes the perpetual struggle between innocence and experience. Because of Dickens's genius, innocence is triumphant in defeat. There have been few writers who have had the kind of genius that is able to give victory to the loser. Shakespeare and Sterne, and Mrs. Gaskell at times, had it, as well as Dickens, but not many others. If Dickens had written nothing at all after *Pickwick*, his name would even so have been with the immortals.

CHAPTER 4

Doughty Street

Dickens did, however, write a great deal more after *Pick-wick*. It would have been difficult for him not to. The entire reading public of England was ready to buy virtually anything he wrote. Publishers were pressing him to sign contracts on almost any terms. Dickens was married. He knew that he would soon be a father. He needed money.

Most writers set to work on a book, write it, see it published, and then (perhaps after a little rest) start another book. Dickens early formed the habit of starting a second novel before he had finished the first; and sometimes he would start a third before he had finished the first two. For most of his life, Dickens was at work on at least two major literary projects at the same time.

Once Dickens saw that each new installment of *Pickwick* would probably be as popular and successful as the last, he began to think of doing some other writing. He rapidly turned out three pieces for the theater: two farces and a comic opera. They were all successful; they were not great. Later, Dickens earnestly tried to forget their existence.

He then agreed to become the editor, for at least one year, of a magazine called *Bentley's Miscellany*. Having signed this contract, he promptly resigned from his job with the *Chronicle*—a step that caused some bitterness in the offices of the *Chronicle* managers, who saw that they were losing a valuable staff member. He made promises, as well, to write two new novels. One was to be called *Gabriel Vardon*, and was to be published by John Macrone. The other was to be called *Oliver Twist*, to be published in serial form in *Bentley's Miscellany*. *Gabriel Vardon* did not appear until 1841, and by then its title had been changed to *Barnaby Rudge*. The first installment of *Oliver Twist* was published in February, 1837.

Oliver Twist is not much like *Pickwick*. It is a grimmer book, and it tells a more dramatic (or melodramatic) story. Just as famous fathers rarely have famous sons, great sequels have rarely been written to great books. Dickens evidently knew that he must never try to write anything just like *Pickwick* again.

The main difference between *Pickwick* and *Oliver Twist* is that, in *Pickwick*, Dickens is portraying, sketching, narrating only; in *Oliver Twist*, he is openly attacking some of the social ills and abuses of his day. Young Oliver Twist was an orphan from birth. In the England of the 1830's, an orphan's lot was a wretched one. Brought up in workhouses, or running homeless about the streets, most orphans were perpetually cold, hungry, and unloved. Dickens was not backward about detailing their plight. At birth, "Oliver cried lustily. If he could have known that he was an

From Oliver Twist

orphan, left to the tender mercies of churchwardens and overseers, perhaps he would have cried the louder."

A few pages further on, there is one of the most famous scenes in English literature. It is set in the workhouse where Oliver lives. Oliver is nine years old.

The evening arrived; the boys took their places. The master, in his cook's uniform, stationed himself at the copper; his pauper assistants ranged themselves behind him; the gruel was served out; and a long grace was said over the short commons. The gruel disappeared; . . . Oliver . . . child as he was . . . was desperate with hunger and reckless with misery. He rose from the table; and advancing to the master, basin and spoon in hand, said, somewhat alarmed at his own temerity:

"Please, sir, I want some more."

The master was a fat, healthy man; but he turned very pale. He gazed in stupefied astonishment on the small rebel for some seconds, and then clung for support to the copper. The assistants were paralysed with wonder; the boys with fear.

"What!" said the master at length, in a faint voice.

"Please, sir," replied Oliver, "I want some more."

The master aimed a blow at Oliver's head with the ladle; pinioned him in his arms; and shrieked aloud for the beadle.

The board were sitting in solemn conclave, when Mr. Bumble rushed into the room in great excitement, and addressing the gentleman in the high chair, said,

"Mr. Limbkins, I beg your pardon, sir! Oliver Twist has asked for more!"

There was a general start. Horror was depicted on every countenance.

"For *more!*" said Mr. Limbkins. "Compose yourself, Bumble, and answer me distinctly. Do I understand that he asked for more, after he had eaten the supper allotted by the dietary?"

"He did, sir," replied Bumble.

"That boy will be hung," said the gentleman in the white waistcoat. "I know that boy will be hung."

Here again, we see what is sad and what is funny blended indissolubly into one. Dickens is teaching us and preaching at us, but he is doing it in such a way that we hardly know that we are being given a lesson. Dickens makes us laugh, but he does not simply tell us a clever little joke that we soon forget. He is writing with power and with color. He is telling us about the life of just one boy: Oliver Twist. But as we read, Oliver becomes every unloved and every forgotten orphan in the world. The Latin expression *Castigat ridendo mores* (Reform the ways of the world by laughter) describes what Dickens wanted to do in most of the books that he wrote after *Pickwick*. We laugh again and again when we read Dickens, but if we have "the eye to see deep enough," we find "dark, fateful, silent elements, tragical to look upon . . . the elements of death itself." There is a straight line in *Oliver Twist* that takes us from the birth of Oliver to the brutal murder of Nancy and the death of Sikes at the end.

33

On January 6, 1837, Dickens became the father of a son. The boy was named Charles (for his father) Culliford (for Dickens's grandparents on his mother's side) Boz (because John Dickens had shouted out "Boz!" at the baby's baptism, when the minister had asked what the baby's name was to be). In March, 1837, the little family was settled in a large and pleasant house at 48 Doughty Street, London.

The family consisted of not only Dickens and his wife Catherine and their baby boy, but also Mary Hogarth, Catherine's sister. Mary Hogarth was a pretty and sweet-natured girl of sixteen. She helped Catherine take care of the baby and do her housework; she adored her new and famous brother-in-law. Dickens was glad to have Mary living with them. For one thing, although Catherine was an attractive and good-tempered person, she was by no means an efficient housekeeper. For another thing, Dickens delighted in the kind of silent admiration that Mary Hogarth felt for him. Perhaps his nature "needed" this admiration because Maria Beadnell had denied it to him in spite of his love for her.

This state of bliss was not to last. On a Saturday night in May of 1837, Dickens, Catherine, and Mary all went to the theater together. They got home at about one o'clock. Mary said good-night, and went upstairs to go to bed. Dickens heard her door close, and then immediately heard a strange, stifled sort of choking noise. He rushed to her room. Mary had had a seizure or an attack of some kind. A doctor was sent for. He could do nothing. At three o'clock in the afternoon of the next day, Mary died.

Dickens was thunderstruck. The death of a beautiful girl

is always one of the saddest things in the world. The death of his young sister-in-law, who adored him in just the way he needed to be adored, was almost unbearable to Dickens. He took a ring from Mary's finger, put it on, and wore it for the rest of his life. He dreamed of her vividly and painfully for many years. In letters that he wrote to friends, he said of Mary more than once, "I solemnly believe that so perfect a creature never breathed . . . she had not a single fault." T 1511803

In spite of his sorrow, Dickens kept on working. He postponed only the May installments of *Pickwick* and *Oliver Twist*. By the end of the year, he had made arrangements to write still another novel: *Nicholas Nickleby*. He was now under contract to three publishers at once: Chapman & Hall, Bentley, and Macrone. During 1838, he worked on *Oliver Twist* and *Nicholas Nickleby* simultaneously; he edited *Bentley's Miscellany*; he wrote some sketches for Chapman & Hall; and he rewrote, for Bentley, the life of Grimaldi, the famous circus clown. As well, because he had become one of the brilliant young literary lions of London, he felt obliged to go to a great many of the banquets and parties to which he was invited. His energy seemed inextinguishable.

By the end of 1838, Dickens had met and talked to most of the famous people in London. Five years before, a rather pompous bank manager had thought that Dickens was not a fit companion for his daughter. Now, whenever he walked down the street, people stopped to stare at him. At public dinners, he was applauded to the rafters by the guests and the waiters both. At small parties, actors, writers, doctors, lords, and bishops jostled one another to be able to shake his hand.

There was Samuel Rogers, the now seventy-five-year-old banker and poet, who had himself met Boswell and Dr. Johnson and the great actor David Garrick. There was Leigh Hunt, who had been a friend of Byron and Shelley and Keats— and who, by saying "no" to Chapman & Hall, had helped to give Dickens the chance to write *Pickwick Papers*. There was Walter Savage Landor, who wrote both poetry and prose, and whose middle name so aptly described his temper. There was Edward Bulwer Lytton, the gaunt, eccentric, hawklike novelist and dramatist and member of Parliament. Until a few years ago every English-speaking child had read Lytton's *The Last Days of Pompeii* at least once. Above all, there were three persons who were to remain his close friends for many years: Angela Burdett Coutts, William Macready, and John Forster.

Angela Burdett Coutts was a well-educated and very rich girl of twenty-one when Dickens first met her. More than anything else, she wanted to use her wealth to help the poor, to help lessen some of the social misery she saw everywhere she turned. Dickens immediately recognized in her a kindred spirit. Until the end of his life, he remained not only her friend, but her trusted adviser and guide. He gave her much good advice on how she might best use her money to improve schools, clean up slums, and ease the lives of the orphan children of London. She trusted him implicitly, and he admired her generosity and high-mindedness; but never for a minute did either of them fall in love with the other. They remained what it is not often easy to find: a man and a woman of nearly the same age, and with similar interests, who were simply good friends.

William Macready was an actor, perhaps the greatest Shakespearean actor of his day. He was forty-four years old, and Dickens was twenty-five, when they met. Their friendship was to last until Dickens's death, and in all that time the two men never quarreled or exchanged any hard words. This was all the more remarkable in that Dickens, although he was not quarrelsome, did have a quick temper and a sharp tongue, and sometimes, in the heat of a moment, he said things that made even his good friends wince with anger.

The fame of an actor rarely outlives him. The names of only a few actors (and actresses) have become part of history: Richard Burbage and Edward Alleyn, the great actors of Shakespeare's time; David Garrick; Sarah Bernhardt, the great French actress, and Eleonora Duse, the great Italian; Ruth Draper, the monologuist who did her sketches in French, Italian, Russian, and German, as well as English. Their names will doubtless be remembered for centuries. William Macready, great actor though he must have been, is now chiefly recalled not for his acting itself, but because he was one of the two principal figures involved in the sad and extraordinary Astor Place riots in New York in 1849.

Macready, then a man of fifty-five, arrived in the United States in 1848. He was considered to be the greatest English-speaking actor alive, save possibly for the fiery

American actor Edwin Forrest. Macready and Forrest, not unnaturally, admired each other's ability and were quite prepared to be friendly rivals. Political feeling and false sentiments of national pride, however, made their appearance. What ought to have been a serious artistic contest between Macready and Forrest degenerated into a massive and bloody brawl.

Both men had been scheduled to appear on May 7, 1849, as Macbeth. Forrest was to play at the Park Theater, and Macready was to play at the Astor Place Theater. Feeling ran high against the Englishman. Outside the Astor Place Theater, and inside it, there were shouts of "Down with the English!" and "Hurrah for native talent!" Macready tried to finish his performance in spite of a rain of eggs and vegetables that landed on the stage; but when, at the beginning of Act III, chairs began to be hurled at him, he not unwisely suspended the performance, and made hasty plans backstage to return immediately to England. Washington Irving and Herman Melville, among many others, embarrassed for what had happened, prevailed upon him to change those plans and do the play again. On May 10, Macready once more walked onstage at the Astor Place Theater as Macbeth. Police lined the walls inside the auditorium, and Macready managed to finish the performance. Outside the theater, a crowd of twenty thousand swirled about the streets, threatening to burn the building down and stone the patrons (and Macready) as they emerged. Troops were called. They, in turn, were attacked by the mob. The troops responded with shots. Thirty-one persons died of wounds, or in the panic that ensued. Macready was hurried to Boston in disguise, and there quickly boarded a ship for England. Nothing like it had happened before, or has happened since, in the history of the theater.

John Forster, Dickens's third close friend, was a swarthy, chunky, bulldog of a man. He is remembered today, if at all, because he had known Dickens so well, and because he wrote a biography of him. Nothing would displease Forster more, if he could look in on today's world, than to know that his fame has now vanished entirely, save for a few beams of reflected glory. In his own day, Forster was "somebody." He thought that he was "somebody," and many other people thought that he was, too. He was the editor of several magazines; he was a professional critic of literature and drama; he wrote biographies of several men other than Dickens, including Goldsmith and Landor. Today, he is virtually "nobody." Little of anything that he wrote (except his life of Dickens) is read by anyone nowadays, save by those in search of literary curiosities. His opinions on many subjects were widely quoted in England during his lifetime. They are never referred to today.

Forster had a great many public and social faults. He was a snob. He was pompous. He was a name-dropper. He often drank too much. He was rude to people that he considered to be of no importance, and servile to people that he thought were important. He tirelessly sought out the famous, ingratiated himself with them, and then dropped the friendship if they did not accept his every opinion and suggestion. He was loud. He was a gossip. He was a boor. But this was only the public John Forster. When he was alone with one or two friends, he became quite suddenly a different man. He was quiet, kind, generous, understanding, patient, and ready to be of real help with any sort of problem. It was, of course, this second, private Forster that was the good friend of Macready and of Robert Browning and of Dickens. Many of us change a little in much this way. Many of us are somewhat different in public from the way we are in private. Forster seemed to be two separate and distinct men. His night-and-day character was the exasperation and the despair of everyone who knew him.

Shortly after Dickens and Forster had first met, late in 1836, the generous, understanding, and helpful side of Forster was called to the fore. Dickens badly needed a wise, kind friend. His finances and his contracts with publishers were in a state of great confusion. Forster proved to be a friend in need. It took him several years to do it, but he finally set Dickens's business affairs in order.

It was not that Dickens was a bad businessman. It was rather that the market value of his writings had gone up rapidly and markedly, and was continuing to go up. Dickens did not know how to deal with his developing popularity. In the spring of 1836, he was glad to sign a contract to write a novel for which he would be paid £200. In the summer of 1836, because *Pickwick* had proved so popular, he signed another contract (with Richard Bentley, the proprietor of *Bentley's Miscellany*) to write two novels and be paid £500 for each. In November, 1836, when Bentley offered Dickens the job as editor of his magazine, the two men agreed on a basic salary of £20 a month. In March, 1837, just four months later, Dickens's salary was increased to £30 a month.

The problem that Forster had to face was not purely a money matter. To a large extent, it was a moral problem. Dickens was becoming aware—as were other people—that "his books 'were enriching everyone connected with them' except himself." For example, Chapman & Hall had made a profit of £20,000 from *Pickwick*. Dickens had earned £2,500. Was this fair? Should the men that print, bind, and distribute a book make nearly ten times more money from it than the man that writes it? At the same time, it must be remembered that although *Pickwick* had been a success, publishers often find that they print, bind, and distribute a book, and no one will buy it. Then they lose a great deal of money.

Forster was obliged to face this question, and several others. For example: a man signs a contract to write a novel, and to be paid $2,000 for it. Within a year, things change. Now any publisher would pay him $5,000 for a novel. What is the writer's moral position? Must he abide by the original $2,000 contract? Or should he try to get out of it?

Dickens was in a position not unlike this one. The publishers—Bentley, in particular—wanted him to honor the old contracts. Dickens wanted the old contracts broken or altered. Forster went back and forth between Bentley and Dickens, and between Dickens and Chapman & Hall. Finally, in June, 1840, an agreement was reached. Contracts and money changed hands. Bentley relinquished all rights in Dickens's work. Chapman & Hall were to be his sole publishers. Naturally, Dickens felt grateful to Forster for what he had done.

41

On March 6, 1838, Dickens's and Catherine's second child was born. She was a girl whom they named Mary. Dickens had been at work, by then, on his third novel for just a month. That novel was *Nicholas Nickleby*. It proved to be an immediate popular favorite. Fifty thousand copies of the first installment were sold. *Nicholas Nickleby* has not, however, lasted quite as well as some of Dickens's other novels. *Oliver Twist*, in spite of a number of heavy-handedly melodramatic pages, remains one of the touchstones of English literature. Oliver himself, Mr. Bumble, Fagin's lessons on how to steal, the Artful Dodger, even Bill Sikes and Nancy, although their brutal doings are told in a reserved and sober language that has now gone out of style—we remember these long after we have shut the book. In the same way, *Nickleby* has its gallery of colorful people—Mr. Mantalini, with his impossibly exquisite way of talking; Mrs. Nickleby, who was a partial portrait of Dickens's own mother; Sir Mulberry Hawk; and Smike; and the Squeers family. The *Nickleby* characters are colorful; they are not brilliant. They do not imprint themselves on our memory as deeply as the characters in *Oliver Twist*. *Nicholas Nickleby* has breadth and sweep and it is, perhaps, funnier than *Oliver Twist*. But it does not have as much imaginative depth.

Dickens's original intention in writing *Nickleby* was, in every way, a praiseworthy one. He wanted to attack the badly run schools of his day. There were schools in England in 1837 where the students (usually orphans sent as year-round boarding students by relatives who did not want to, or could not, take care of them) put in long days of manual

Charles Dickens. age 27

labor, were fed on all but rotten food and were obliged to sleep five in one flea-infested bed. Dickens did a little research on such schools before starting *Nicholas Nickleby*. He saw an "academy" in Yorkshire, run by a man named Shaw. The graveyard nearby told him nearly everything that he needed to know, for twenty-five boys between the ages of seven and eighteen had been buried there in twenty-four years. It was Dickens's hope to be able to do something to correct that kind of vicious situation. Undoubtedly, *Nickleby* did accomplish something. Such schools have all but vanished since those days, and doubtless Dickens's novel was in part responsible for their disappearance.

The excellence of a novel, however, is not measured entirely by the amount of good it accomplishes in the field of social reform. Novels do have a social, a crusading, function; but if their whole purpose, the entire reason for their existence, were to crusade, to change and improve the world we live in, novels would be essays and not novels at all. A novel must have a story to tell, must contain characters that speak to us, must make us laugh or thrill or cry. A novel is a reflection and a re-creation of many aspects of society. Social reform is only one aspect of society, one of man's many interests and duties and desires.

Nicholas Nickleby has not lasted as well as *Oliver Twist*, perhaps because Dickens, in 1836 and 1837, was simply trying to write too much. A reviewer named Abraham Hayward made this point in an article in the *Quarterly*, in October, 1837: "Mr. Dickens writes too often and too fast."

From one point of view, he may have been right.

CHAPTER 5

Devonshire Terrace

The character of Dickens's father did not change much during the years in which Dickens was becoming England's most famous writer. John Dickens remained as good-natured and sociable as ever, and just as irresponsible about money. He was still perpetually in debt, but now he thought that he had found a new way to raise a little cash. With no malice at all in his heart, he took to selling specimens of his son's handwriting to the curious; and he would stop in, now and then, at Chapman & Hall's offices to borrow "a trifling sum" from his son's publishers.

After a time, Dickens found out about his amiable parent's activities. Something had to be done. He decided to rent a small house in a town away from London, and set his parents up in it. In March, 1839, he found near Exeter a cottage that he thought would do very well. It was small, trim, and white; it had a flower garden and a vegetable garden; it had a view of the towers of Exeter Cathedral in the distance. There John Dickens and his wife went to live for several years.

Charles Dickens and his family moved about this time, too. A third child was born in October, 1839, a girl that was named Kate Macready. The house in Doughty Street was now too small for them. Dickens found a handsome new house at 1 Devonshire Terrace, not far from where the Macreadys lived. By December, 1839, the move had been made. In Devonshire Terrace, Dickens was to write some of his most famous works, including *David Copperfield*, *A Christmas Carol*, and *The Old Curiosity Shop*.

Dickens started *The Old Curiosity Shop* in 1840. *Pickwick* and *Twist* and *Nickleby* had been both successful and popular. *The Old Curiosity Shop* electrified the English-speaking world. The novel tells the story of Little Nell Trent and her grandfather. They run the Old Curiosity Shop, but a cruel moneylender named Quilp seizes the shop, and they are forced to flee London. The old man and the child have many adventures and meet many strange people as they wander about England from town to town, hoping to find a place where they can settle down safely and comfortably. At last they do find a pleasant village; but now, sick and worn-out, both of them die.

The death of Little Nell reduced nearly all of Dickens's readers to an agony of grief. The general consensus was that no writing so glorious and so tragic as this had been done in English since Shakespeare. In New York, anxious crowds lined the pier to meet the ship that was bringing in the final installment. In Colorado and in Texas, miners and ranch hands wept unashamedly over the last pages. Daniel O'Connell read the final chapters of the book while he was taking a train trip. When he came to the part about

46

The Old Curiosity Shop, immortalized by Dickens, is still a favorite tourist stop.

Nell's death, he threw the book out of the train window and burst into tears.

In spite of all the furor, all the grief, and all the tears that it caused, *The Old Curiosity Shop* has not really survived. What has happened? What has changed? Why do so many readers today yawn at the very parts of the book that a century ago made thousands weep?

It is partly because when Dickens was thirty years old, deathbed scenes in novels were all the rage. Today the reading public likes love stories better than any other kind. A hundred years ago, love stories, as we have them now, were not nearly so popular. It was considered bad taste to write about the things that a man might say and do when he was alone with the woman he was in love with. If a writer had described the embraces and the tenderest whispered conversations of a couple in love, he would have been condemned for "peeking," for taking liberties with people's privacy. There was much more interest in the last moments before a person died. Life was shorter then, more painful and more dangerous. Before he reached the age of ten, nearly every child had helped to bury at least three or four of his close relatives and friends. By the time he was thirty, a man had seen die a dozen or more people that he had known very well. The whole subject of death was terrifying, immediate, and compelling in a way that it is not today.

Death was inevitably on Dickens's mind while he was writing *The Old Curiosity Shop*. He had just seen Mary Hogarth die, suddenly and inexplicably, when she was only sixteen. He changed and re-created Mary in his imagination, and she came forth as Nell. When Little Nell died, the English-speaking world shared with him the grief that he had felt for Mary's death.

The Old Curiosity Shop satisfied the needs and the tastes of its times. Needs and tastes since then have changed, and poor Little Nell seems somewhat embarrassing and out of place to us. Many of the things that Dickens wrote were "for all time." *The Old Curiosity Shop* was powerful and apt when it appeared, but it was only "of an age."

In July, 1840, Dickens had an experience that troubled him greatly. He went to a public hanging. In England, and in many countries of the world, the execution of criminals used to be a public event. The spectacle of a guilty man's death would, it was thought, frighten many people away from ever breaking the law. Public executions, of course, did not have any such purifying effect. Even among the very crowd that gathered to witness the hanging of a thief, there were always a large number of other thieves and pickpockets, picking away at pockets as fast as they could. Finally, the law understood. It was decided that public executions were savage and brutal spectacles, and they were discontinued.

What shocked Dickens about the hanging that he viewed (of a murderer named François Courvoisier), was not only the painful sadness of seeing a life snuffed out but also the hardheartedness, the nearly sadistic attitude of the crowd. Many of the spectators had waited all night to have a good, front-row place near the scaffold. When the unfortunate Courvoisier appeared—terrified, trying to pray—the mob shouted abuse and obscenities at him. When the rope broke Courvoisier's neck, a great bloodthirsty roar went up.

Dickens knew, as everyone knows, that murderers must be restrained, and kept from doing further violence. Whether murder could ever be stamped out by murdering the murderers, Dickens was not so sure. But he *was* certain that making a circus of capital punishment was wrong. He was disappointed, as well, to see that the mob of spectators gave no evidence of sorrow or fear or sympathy. They simply howled and roared with savage delight.

A year after the hanging of Courvoisier, Dickens met a crowd under very different circumstances. He was invited to go to Edinburgh and to be the guest of honor at a banquet which took place on June 25, 1841. Five hundred people were in the hall. When Dickens walked in to take his place, the band played *Charlie is My Darlin'*, and every person present stood and cheered. After the meal, several speeches were made, and Dickens spoke, too, thanking his hosts and the people of Edinburgh. Four days after the dinner, he was officially given the "freedom of the city of Edinburgh." Before he had turned thirty, Dickens was one of the most celebrated and beloved men in Great Britain.

By a strange coincidence, Dickens received this first great public acclamation in his life—he was to receive much more before he died—at the very time that he was at work on one of his weakest and least successful novels. *Barnaby Rudge* (originally to have been known as *Gabriel Vardon*) had been planned and contracted for several years earlier. Dickens had not got around to writing it, and it had been a nagging source of worry to him, something that had to be done, but that he could not bring himself to get down to. The first installment of it finally appeared in February, 1841.

Most critics and readers today agree that *Rudge* shows evidence of strain. It is clear to the reader that the author took little pleasure in writing the book. When it came out, *Rudge* was not nearly as popular as Dickens's other novels had been. Edgar Allan Poe wrote a review of it, saying that it was good, but less good than the *Curiosity Shop*. And in another article published in May, 1841, after only eleven chapters of *Rudge* had appeared, Poe predicted, on the basis of what had already been written, how the novel must end. Dickens was greatly surprised, and perhaps just a little bit put out, when he heard about the article, because Poe had been entirely right in at least some of his predictions. *Barnaby Rudge* may have served Poe in another way, too. There is a raven in the book, named Grip, that Dickens put there partly because he had a pet raven himself while he was doing the writing. In 1845, Poe put such a bird into his own most famous poem, *The Raven*.

During the year 1841, Dickens rather suddenly decided that he wanted to visit America. The trip from England to America was not an easy one in the 1840's; and travel in the United States and Canada was slow and anything but pleasurable. Catherine, not unnaturally, did not like the idea of the journey. In fact, "Kate cries dismally if I mention the subject," Dickens wrote in a letter to Forster. Just why Dickens wanted to go, in spite of his wife's objections, and the discomforts that he knew that the trip would entail, is not clear, but the plans went forward. It was arranged that the children—there were four now—would stay with the Macreadys. On January 4, 1842, Dickens and Catherine sailed from Liverpool for America, aboard the S.S. *Britannia*. They did not know it, but they were entering one of the most difficult and unhappy periods of their lives. All in all, it probably would have been better if they had not gone.

CHAPTER 6

America

Transatlantic liners nowadays are of anywhere from 12,000 to 80,000 tons. The *Britannia* was 1,150 tons. The Atlantic Ocean was stormier, during the month of January, 1842, than it had been for years. For half of the voyage, Catherine and Dickens lay in their berths in their tiny cabin, wretched with seasickness. On the several occasions that they did go to the dining room, the rolling and pitching of the ship was so severe that they, and all the other passengers, were periodically hurled out of their chairs and sent helplessly sprawling. Finally, after fourteen days, the sea grew calm, and on Thursday, January 20, the *Britannia* put in at Halifax, Nova Scotia. She lay over there for a few hours, during which Dickens was entertained by the governor of the province, and then set sail for Boston. The trip was finally over on January 22. Dickens and Catherine disembarked, and were greeted by an enthusiastic group of people that had come down to the pier to meet them.

All his life Dickens loved public attention and the applause of the crowd. The boisterous welcome given him by the city of Boston, and later by every American city that he visited, was, however, too much even for him. If he went out for a walk in the streets, crowds followed him, gawking. The lobbies of the hotels that he stayed in were constantly full of all kinds of people that wanted to shake his hand or cut snips from his clothes, or his hair, for souvenirs. He received ten times more invitations to receptions and dinners than he could possibly have accepted. His sleep was frequently interrupted by curious crowds milling about noisily beneath his hotel windows.

Dickens had been prepared to like America, and America had been prepared to like Dickens. Both were quickly disenchanted. Perhaps strangely, many Americans, when they had seen him in the flesh, thought that Dickens was flashy and vulgar, and not at all the personification of the fine moral force they had expected. In his turn, Dickens thought that Americans were ill-mannered and tedious. Dickens's habit of wearing green velvet waistcoats, and of combing his handsome head of hair in public, disturbed conservative Americans. The American habit of chewing tobacco (and spitting) bothered Dickens. Americans had somehow expected Dickens to be a wise, witty, soft-spoken person. They found that their guest was an exuberant boy of thirty years old.

After a few days in Boston, Dickens was obliged to hire a social secretary. The painter Francis Alexander, who did a rather cherubic portrait of Dickens while he was in Boston, suggested George Putnam, a young artist. Putnam immediately went to work trying to arrange a feasible schedule for his famous employer. It turned out that

Dickens met everyone in America "worth knowing." In Boston, he was introduced to Longfellow, the poet; to Charles Sumner, the statesman; to Richard Henry Dana, Jr., the author of *Two Years Before the Mast*. Dana was, at first, distressed by Dickens. He found him too hearty and offhand, and "far from well-bred." But on closer acquaintance he changed his mind and declared that Dickens was natural and unpretending, "with a face full of light."

A great banquet was given in Boston in Dickens's honor on February 1. One hundred and fifty people were present. An orchestra played during the meal, and several men made speeches praising Dickens. He was a great writer, they said, and a man of true goodness. Finally, Dickens rose to reply. He had intended to say some things of importance. He was surprised to find that what he said struck many people as rude and offensive.

First he said that he was sure that "Virtue shows quite as well in rags and patches, as she does in purple and fine linen." His hearers applauded this noble and democratic sentiment. But then he went on to say this: "I hope the time is not far distant when [writers] in America, will receive of right some substantial profit and return in England for their labors; and when we in England shall receive some substantial profit and return in America from ours. Pray do not misunderstand me . . . I would rather have the affectionate regard of my fellowmen than I would have heaps and mines of gold . . ."

He was referring to the fact that there were not, in those days, any international copyright laws. A writer's books, once printed, could be taken by any foreign publisher (translated, if necessary), and reprinted; and the author would receive not one penny. Dickens's own books had been reprinted in America and read by hundreds of thousands of people, but Dickens had been paid nothing at all by the Americans for what he had written. This was a situation that Dickens thought intolerable. How was an author to live? He spent all his time writing, and what he wrote was, except in his own homeland, simply to be given away. Printers and publishers, of course, made money in America from Dickens's books. Dickens himself did not.

The day after the banquet, the Boston newspapers accused Dickens of gross bad taste. A dinner had been given in his honor, and Dickens, in the course of it, had stood up and asked to be paid. How vulgar, they groaned, to mix business with pleasure in this way!

Dickens being Dickens, the newspaper articles only confirmed his determination to argue for copyright laws at every possible opportunity. On February 5, he left Boston, according to schedule, for New York by way of Hartford and New Haven. At Hartford he was given another grand banquet. At the end of the banquet, he made a speech in which he returned to the copyright theme, and spoke even more vigorously about it than he had in Boston. After this speech, a few people quietly suggested to him that it might be out of place for a guest to talk about money in this way with his hosts. The newspapers, the next day, said that Dickens was abusing hospitality in a most ungentlemanly manner, and declared that the people of the United States "wanted no advice from Mr. Dickens on this subject."

Whether the people of the United States wanted advice

from Mr. Dickens or not, they were going to get it. At a dinner in New York in the middle of February, he returned to the subject. This time, however, he received a little support. The toastmaster at this particular dinner was the well-known author Washington Irving. In proposing the toast to Dickens, Irving had planned to speak in the same breath of "Charles Dickens, the literary guest of the nation, *and* International Copyright." Irving was, however, a shy man, and no public speaker, and he lost his nerve before he had expressed his sentiment. Dickens, nevertheless, rose to his feet, and once again argued for copyright laws. The reaction to what he said was just slightly more favorable than it had been in Hartford and Boston. The *New York Tribune* went so far as to support his position, while the other New York newspapers, instead of attacking him, merely ignored him.

Dickens was by no means alone in his fight to see an international copyright law established. While he was speaking on the subject in America, several men in England, Macaulay among them, were advocating wiser copyright laws of all kinds. Such famous writers as Leigh Hunt, Samuel Rogers, Bulwer-Lytton, and Tennyson publicly supported Dickens's stand. American publishers, however, petitioned Congress to forbid the passage of an international copyright act, and they were, for a time, successful. It was not until 1892 that England and the United States came to an agreement in the matter.

In March, Dickens and Catherine left New York for Philadelphia. There Dickens met and talked with Edgar Allan Poe. From Philadelphia, they went to Baltimore

and Washington. In Washington, they met the most famous politicians and statesmen of the day: John C. Cal-
houn, Daniel Webster, Henry Clay, and President John
Tyler. They had dinner with courtly ex-President John
Quincy Adams, then seventy-six years old, who wrote a
short poem in honor of the occasion and sent it to Catherine. Washington Irving, who was about to leave the
United States in order to take up his duties as minister to
Spain, came down for a farewell dinner. Dickens was flattered by all the attention and praise he was receiving (even
if there was a little too much of it), but he was also disturbed now by something other than the copyright question.

In Washington, Dickens was in the slaveholding region
of the United States, and he was distressed by the phenome-
non of slavery. He argued with men who were advocates
of slavery, and he deplored to them the evils and the cruel-
ties of the system. Of course, he admitted, there were undoubtedly some kind slave owners in the country, who did
their best to see that their slaves lived pleasant, safe, and
even relatively happy lives. Unfortunately though, he
added, there were also cruel slave owners, for abuse of
power is one of the commonest of human failings. History
shows us that there are many thoughtless persons, many
drunkards, and not a few sadists in the world. Under such
owners, the slave's lot is painful, abject, and sad. Slavery
must be abolished, he said. Besides, he inquired of those
persons that told him that most slaves were happy, why
are United States newspapers, then, so full of advertise-
ments asking for the return of runaway slaves?

From Washington, Dickens and Catherine went to Harrisburg, and then to Pittsburgh, where they boarded a river steamer which took them down the Ohio to Cincinnati, a city that Dickens very much liked. From Cincinnati, they went on to Louisville. From Louisville, they went past Cairo, at the confluence of the Ohio and the Mississippi rivers, and north to St. Louis. Missouri was then a slave state, and Dickens once more found himself arguing against slavery.

Dickens was now in a bad mood. Everywhere he went, crowds pressed about him. He could find hardly a minute in which he could, by himself, look relaxedly at the country he had come so far to visit. He was disturbed at the hostile reaction that his well-intentioned remarks about copyright had elicited. He was distressed by the heated arguments he so often heard in favor of slavery. At this point, he grew annoyed, too, perhaps unreasonably, with his long-suffering wife. She had endured all the discomforts of a rugged journey, much of it through frontier country and a "man's world" of drink, tobacco chewing, and bad language, with hardly a murmur. She had, however, a habit that was beginning to get on Dickens's nerves. She was clumsy. She was constantly skidding, sliding, slipping, tripping, stumbling, or falling. Her legs were perpetually scraped. Her shins and elbows were covered with bruises. She fell either into or out of every coach or boat that they used. Dickens, who was always quick and sure of foot, could not hide his displeasure. He began counting, and at the end of their trip he estimated, laughing sourly, that Catherine had tripped or fallen seven hundred and forty-three times in North America. It was the first sign of a rift in their marriage. The rift was to widen.

From St. Louis, they went back by steamer to Cincinnati and then overland to Columbus, Cleveland, and Buffalo. From Buffalo, they took a train to Niagara. Niagara Falls pleased and impressed Dickens more than anything that he had seen so far in the New World. The reason may have been that they stayed at Niagara for a week, and there they were left blessedly to themselves, without banquets, speeches, arguments, or crowds.

After Niagara, they crossed into Canada, and went on to Toronto and to Kingston, which was then the seat of the Canadian government. Dickens liked what he saw of Canada (although he found Toronto a bit too Tory for his tastes), because Canada's ties with the British Crown had kept the country slightly more English than the United States was, and, therefore, he could feel more at home in it. He discovered, too, as he traveled north and east to Montreal, that he very much liked the French-Canadian villages in Quebec. They stayed for several weeks in Montreal, and while they were there, they both took part in some plays that were being put on by a group of amateurs for charity.

Early in June, they were once again in New York. On June 7, they boarded the *George Washington* and sailed for England.

As soon as he was home, Dickens set to work on a book about his trip. All in all, he had not liked America. And he made no great effort to keep his dislike out of his pages.

After all, he must have said to himself, I have often had hard things to say about England, my own country: why should I suddenly change my habits, and write a book praising a social scene that I cannot approve of? What Dickens forgot is that it is one thing for a man to speak ill of his own family, or his own country, or even of himself; it is quite another to speak ill of what is someone else's. Good manners come into the picture here, and in his *American Notes*, Dickens offended against good manners. He wrote harshly against slavery. So far, so good. If he had said nothing else against the United States, he might have been considered to have been criticizing a human ill rather than a national failing. He might have been applauded for his courage by all but the most vigorous anti-abolitionists. Unfortunately, he went on to comment adversely on tobacco-chewing, American business practices, American publishers, American manners, American newspapers, American roads, and other matters. When he did speak well of persons and things, his tone was rather patronizing.

Not surprisingly, *American Notes* was unpopular in America. Dickens was accused by reviewers of being "coarse . . . vulgar . . .childish . . . contemptible." The book was not well received in England, either. Even William Macready owned to not having enjoyed it. Macaulay went so far as to refuse to write a review of it. He knew Dickens personally, he said, and therefore he did not want to "cut up" one of his books, and *American Notes*, Macaulay wrote to a friend, was "on the whole a failure."

A trip that might have turned out to be a success and a pleasure for all concerned ended in disappointment, anger, and bitterness. Perhaps, it was simply that Dickens was too young when he made it.

CHAPTER 7

Italy

Not long after Dickens and Catherine had returned from America, another of Catherine's sisters, Georgina, moved into the house at Devonshire Terrace. Georgina Hogarth was then fifteen years old. She had become "Aunty Georgy" to the Dickens children while their parents had been away. Dickens found that Georgina reminded him strongly of Mary Hogarth. As Mary had, Georgina adored her brother-in-law; and as Mary had been, Georgina was an efficient housekeeper. Catherine was glad to turn at least part of the management of the big Devonshire Terrace house over to her. Dickens basked in the sunlight of her admiration. The children adored their Aunty Georgy. All was well.

Dickens had not inherited many of his father's characteristics, but son and father did have one trait in common: they were both untiringly sociable. Dickens carried his sociability to an even more extraordinary degree than his father had—and he had more money in his pocket with which to do it. Save when he was writing (and then he demanded that he not be disturbed for any reason at all), he did not like to be alone. Indeed, it would be truer to say that he could not stand to be alone. There were always guests for at least one meal a day at Devonshire Terrace; and there were often houseguests, as well, who stayed for days, or even weeks, at a time. Forster, or Macready and his wife, would arrive for dinner. Douglas Jerrold, the dramatist, might come for tea with Mark Lemon, the editor of *Punch*. Augustus Egg, the artist, called frequently over the years, although he probably came more to see Georgina than to see Dickens himself. Longfellow arrived from America and stayed for several days in October, 1842. Samuel Gridley Howe, the director of the Perkins School for the Blind in Boston, and his wife, Julia Ward Howe, the author of the *Battle Hymn of the Republic*, visited him.

Dickens had time for all these people, and time to romp boisterously with his children. It was only for Catherine that he did not seem to have much time. He was a generous and thoughtful husband, but as the years went by, he grew apart from his wife. Catherine did not have her husband's charm and energy and effervescence. Dickens did not seem to be happy or relaxed in her company alone. When they went out together to a dinner or to a party, not a few people whispered their surprise to each other that the lively, energetic Dickens should have such a quiet, listless wife. Dickens himself was doubtless disappointed that his wife turned out not to have as much sparkle and vitality as he had, that she could not "keep up with him." At the same time, he did not do much to try to make her into the kind of companion-wife that he needed and wanted.

After finishing his *American Notes*, Dickens set to work on a novel that he called *Martin Chuzzlewit*—having discarded such names for its hero as Sweezlewag, Chuzzletoe, and Chubblewig.

He thought the novel one of the best that he had written so far. Some of his friends tended to agree with him. (But not all. Macready confided to his diary that "I grieve over it.") A few readers in the twentieth century have gone so far as to call *Chuzzlewit* "the greatest work of comic genius in English literature." Certainly Sairey Gamp, the nurse, is one of the great comic characters in the history of fiction. She is an improbable blend of Dogberry with a decaying Wife of Bath. (She was modeled on a nurse who had, in fact, taken care of a friend of Angela Coutts's.) Her constant appeals to her friend, the ever absent Mrs. Harris, are a stroke of comic genius that few writers have ever equaled. Mrs. Harris exists, and she does not exist. Her entire role in life is to provide wisps of conversation that Mrs. Gamp can later quote to her own credit. Finally, Betsey Prig, Mrs. Gamp's other friend, her tongue loosened by sips from the contents of a teapot that has an odor about it somewhat more fragrant than teapots usually give off, can bear it no longer:

> Mrs. Gamp resumed:
> "Mrs. Harris, Betsey—"
> "Bother Mrs. Harris!" said Betsey Prig.
> Mrs. Gamp looked at her with amazement, incre-

dulity, and indignation; when Mrs. Prig, shutting her eye still closer, and folding her arms still tighter, uttered these memorable and tremendous words:

"I don't believe there's no sich a person!"

After the utterance of which expressions, she leaned forward and snapped her fingers once, twice, thrice; each time nearer to the face of Mrs. Gamp, and then rose to put on her bonnet, as one who felt that there was now a gulf between them, which nothing could ever bridge across.

The shock of this blow was so violent and sudden, that Mrs. Gamp sat staring at nothing with uplifted eyes, and her mouth open as if she were gasping for breath, until Betsey Prig had put on her bonnet and her shawl, and was gathering the latter about her throat. Then Mrs. Gamp rose—morally and physically rose—and denounced her.

"What!" said Mrs. Gamp, "you bage creetur, have I know'd Mrs. Harris five and thirty year, to be told at last that there ain't no sech a person livin'! Have I stood her friend in all her troubles, great and small, for it to come at last to sech a end as this . . ."

Mrs. Gamp, later, can say only:

". . . wot I have took from Betsey Prig this blessed night, no mortial creetur knows! If she had abuged me, bein' in liquor, which I thought I smelt her wen she come, but could not so believe, not bein' used myself"—Mrs. Gamp, by the way, was pretty far gone, and the fragrance of the teapot was strong in the room— " I could have bore it with a thankful art. But the words she spoke of Mrs. Harris, lambs could not forgive. No. Betsey!" said Mrs. Gamp, in a violent burst of feeling, "nor worms forget!"

Dickens's original intention in *Martin Chuzzlewit* was to laugh at individual human vices, in much the way that in *Pickwick* he had laughed at individual human eccentricities and virtues. He had even planned to preface the novel with a motto: "Your homes the scene, yourselves the actors, here!" but Forster persuaded him to abandon the idea. It was only after 1850 that Dickens was to write entire novels analyzing and criticizing not individuals but society as a whole. After he had written fifteen chapters of *Chuzzlewit*, however, Dickens took his first steps toward the adoption of a general, rather than the particular, view of life. The use of these two different methods in one novel, can, perhaps, account for the somewhat loosely-put-together plot of *Chuzzlewit*.

The reading public of the 1840's did not seem to like *Martin Chuzzlewit* as much as they had liked Dickens's earlier novels. The sales of its first installments reached only about twenty thousand copies a month. Dickens, who was never able to keep his eye off sales charts, decided that he must do something. What he did was to send Martin, in the novel, to America. He evidently felt that more remarks and complaints about America as a whole, would increase the popularity of the book, at least in England.

They did not. Sales went up, but only by about three or

four thousand. English readers seemed to want tales of virtue in distress, similar to the pathetic history of Little Nell. Readers in the United States set up a fresh, angry outcry against Dickens. Slaveholders were especially loud in their condemnation of the book. They could hardly have been expected to have remained calm when they read such passages as this:

"He went," said Mrs. Lupin, with increased distress, "to America. He was always tenderhearted and kind, and perhaps at this moment may be lying in prison under sentence of death, for taking pity on some miserable black, and helping the poor runaway creetur to escape. How could he ever go to America! Why didn't he go to some of those countries where the savages eat each other fairly, and give an equal chance to every one!"

Letters of abuse by the hundred were sent to Dickens by indignant American readers. They did not improve his mood. But worse was yet to come.

Chapman & Hall had advanced Dickens the money with which to pay for his trip to America. At the same time, he had signed an agreement with them to the effect that he would be paid £200 a month for his next novel—which turned out to be *Chuzzlewit*—unless after the first five months it was found that the sales of the novel were not high enough to repay the money that they had advanced. If sales were not high enough, Dickens's payment would be cut to £150 a month. Such was the contract to which

Chapman & Hall and Dickens had put their names. One day in June, 1843, William Hall referred casually, in Dickens's hearing, to the fact that *Chuzzlewit* was not selling very well. He added, in a low voice, that he hoped it would not prove necessary to cut Dickens's pay to the agreed upon £150. Dickens was, by then, already smarting under the fear that he had lost his grip, that he could no longer write books that had a wide popular appeal. When he heard Hall's words, he "promptly went through at least two ceilings, the roof, and well into mid-air." Nor did his rage subside within a day or two. He continued, for several years, to feel only wrath and contempt for his former friends. Three years before, Bentley had been a brigand. Now Chapman and Hall were incompetents, Dickens said. They were "preposterously ignorant of all the essentials of their business." With Forster's help, again, Dickens made plans to have his books published, in the future, by the firm of Bradbury & Evans.

In spite of his bad mood and his anger, Dickens was able to write, in November, 1843, *A Christmas Carol*, the book that may be his most famous piece of writing.

There are not many people in the world who do not know about Scrooge (and his comment on Christmas: "Bah! Humbug!") and Marley's Ghost and poor Bob Cratchit and Tiny Tim, who says "God bless us, every one!" And there are not many who have not rejoiced at the change of heart that comes about in Scrooge:

"A merry Christmas, Bob!" said Scrooge, with an earnestness that could not be mistaken, as he clapped him on the back. "A merrier Christmas, Bob, my good fellow, than I have given you for many a year! I'll raise your salary, and endeavour to assist your struggling family, and we will discuss your affairs this very afternoon, over a Christmas bowl of smoking bishop, Bob! Make up the fires, and buy another coal-scuttle before you dot another i, Bob Cratchit!"

Scrooge was better than his word. He did it all, and infinitely more . . .

Dickens's *Christmas Carol* has become very nearly as much a part of the world's celebration of Christmas as "Silent Night, Holy Night," Christmas trees, and Santa Claus himself.

The tale is well told. It is simple and direct. Its message is obvious and unblushing. Dickens was appealing openly to the sentiments of his readers. He put snow and crackling fires, good food and good drink into Christmas; and there they have stayed. It is true that he was not the first writer to describe the spirit and the activities that have been referred to ever since as "Christmas Cheer"—Washington Irving, several years earlier, had written merrily of Merry Christmases—but Dickens's magic touch succeeded, and took hold of the public imagination, where Irving had only half succeeded.

The *Christmas Carol* is deservedly popular. There is a certain magic about it that makes it irresistible. At the same time, it is true that Dickens not only put snow and crackling fires and food into Christmas, but he put money into it, too. As the story is told, evil is equated with stingi-

The Cratchits' Christmas dinner, from A Christmas Carol

ness, sorrow with poverty, and happiness with prosperity. "I'll raise your salary" are the words by which Scrooge's conversion is indicated, and "Scrooge was better than his word. He did it all, and infinitely more."

It is easy to see that Dickens gave money (and stinginess and generosity) such an important place in the *Carol*, because while he was writing it he was so angry with Chapman & Hall for what he considered their tightfistedness. But the root of Dickens's constant preoccupation with money did not lie entirely in his anger with his former publishers. Many of the books that Dickens wrote before 1843, and after, are concerned with poverty and riches, with the coming into prosperity of a poor but honest and deserving person. *A Tale of Two Cities* does not have this money thread running so clearly through it, but *Little Dorrit* has, and so have *David Copperfield*, *Hard Times*, *Bleak House*, and other Dickens novels, besides.

Dickens wanted his books to have a wide audience. He wanted to write novels that would be read by both the rich businessman and the poor boy that cleaned his carriage house. Prosperity and poverty were two subjects that were much in the public consciousness in the Victorian Age. Minerals taken from vast tracts of land in the United States and Canada and Australia were making some people richer, it seemed, than once they would ever have hoped. Railroads and factories, right in England, were making other men rich, while unjust laws, depressed working conditions, and famines (particularly in Ireland) were making many men poor. England and all Europe were still ringing with the opening sentences of Rousseau's *Social Con-*

tract: "Man is born free, and everywhere he is in chains. Many men believe themselves to be masters of others. . . ."

Dickens was addressing his books both to those that believed themselves masters and to the others. In his novels, he usually did not preach any particular kind of political reform or change in economic practices. He simply urged each single man to live in peace and charity with his neighbor. If, sometimes, the charity seemed to be too emphatically money charity, that is understandable, since money was (and is) such a frequent topic of conversation among all kinds of people. In any case, Count Leo Tolstoy, the Russian novelist, moralist, and theologian, considered Dickens's *Christmas Carol* to be an example of the very highest art— art "flowing from God and man" and knowing no boundaries of upper and lower social class divisions.

The *Christmas Carol* did not make as much money for Dickens as he had hoped that it would. He had expected it to earn him £1,000. He made just about half that figure from it. Now he found himself in serious financial straits, at war with his publishers, the author of a novel that he considered his best (*Chuzzlewit*) but that few people were buying, and the object of the anger and dislike of a large number of Americans.

It was the last straw when he found that a small publishing company named Lee and Haddock had printed and were illegally distributing copies of the *Christmas Carol*. He decided to apply for a court injunction to stop them. The case was heard, and the injunction was granted. Dickens then sued for damages. Lee and Haddock promptly declared bankruptcy. Dickens not only did not obtain damages, but he was obliged to pay £700 to cover the court costs.

Disappointed and angry, Dickens decided to leave England for a year. Perhaps the sun and wine of Italy would do him good. Even if they did not, it would be cheaper to live in Italy than it would be to live in England.

Having jettisoned Chapman & Hall, Dickens quickly came to terms with Bradbury & Evans. They agreed to lend him £2,800. He agreed to let them have, in return, a fourth share in all the writing that he might do in the next eight years.

On July 2, 1844, the Dickens family set out in a vast coach that Dickens had bought: Catherine, Georgina, the children—Charley, Mamie, Katie, Walter, and Frank, who was just six months old—Catherine's maid, Anne, Louis Roche, who was to act as driver and as Dickens's valet, several other servants, and a white spaniel named Timber. After a time, Dickens's mood of depression passed, and he began looking forward with enthusiasm to his Italian year.

It is interesting to notice how many famous men and women in history have spent long periods of time in Italy—Milton, Gray, Mozart, Byron, Shelley, Keats, Mendelssohn, Goethe, Ruskin, Stendhal, Ibsen, the Brownings. It is, perhaps, easier to make a list of those that have *not* been to Italy. For centuries, hundreds of thousands of people have been drawn there like filings to a magnet, and they still are drawn today. Why? Is it because of the vivid blue of the sky, and the brightness of the sunshine? Is it because of the food and the wine? Because of the voluble, happy, lovable nature of the Italian people? The beautiful architecture? The great paintings? The splendid and touching ruins of ancient Rome—"the grandeur that was Rome?" It is because of all these things, certainly, and more besides. For some mysterious, inexplicable reason, a man feels more like a man when he is in Italy than he has ever felt in his life, and a woman feels more like a woman. Going to Italy is like growing up all over again. One suddenly feels that one has had a revelation of what life is really all about. Italy may not be quite the earthly paradise of the civilized world, but it is the closest thing to it that there is. There is an Italian phrase that says, *"Ma l'Italia è un'altra cosa"*—"But Italy is something else again." And so it is.

The Dickenses traveled south through France, from Paris to Lyon, to Avignon, to Marseilles. At Marseilles, they boarded a ship that took them to Genoa. A house had been rented for them at Albaro, a suburb of Genoa. The house proved to be a grim disappointment. It was like a house in a tale by Edgar Allan Poe. The rooms were huge and cheerless. The furniture was comfortless and unwieldy. The garden was a menagerie of fleas, flies, lizards, scorpions, frogs, and stray cats. The sun that blazed into the building during the day was of a fierce heat that no one in the family had expected. For several days, even Dickens, with all his physical energy, could not adjust to this dramatic change in surroundings. He reported that his tendency upon getting up in the morning was, at first, simply "to tumble down anywhere and lie there."

Gradually, he did adjust. He wandered all over Genoa on foot. He took some Italian lessons, and began to read Manzoni's *The Betrothed* in the original. He discovered a delightful marionette theater where the marionettes did, among other things, a dramatization of the death of Napoleon Bonaparte. As the Napoleon marionette slowly expired, the doctor marionette attending him, Dickens later wrote, because of "some derangement of his wires, hovered about the couch like a vulture, and gave medical opinions in the air."

The Albaro house, barely inhabitable during the summer, would have decimated the family during the winter. Luckily, Dickens found that the second floor of the huge Peschiere Palace in the city of Genoa itself was unoccupied and for rent. In September, the whole household moved into it. Below them, on the ground floor, lived a Spanish nobleman and his lady, with their six daughters and infant son.

The Peschiere Palace, or Fishpond Palace (Palazzo Peschiere in Italian), was one of the most beautiful houses in Genoa, a city famous for its many beautiful buildings. The Dickenses were as delighted with it, and with the view of the harbor and the massive lighthouse in the distance, as they had been displeased with the house at Albaro. Even so, it was not until the second week of October that Dickens could settle down to work. Then, suddenly, he was seized by a "ferocious excitement to write." For days he had been bothered by the constant ringing of the church bells that was part of the way of life of Genoa. Finally, there came into his mind the famous line spoken by Falstaff in Shakespeare's *Henry IV*, *Part Two:* "We have heard the chimes at midnight, Master Shallow." From that moment on, he had a story, and he had a title for it: *The Chimes.*

As he wrote, Dickens became more and more convinced that he was writing one of the best things that he had ever done. It was a short work, no longer than the *Christmas Carol*, and he wanted to have it published, like the *Christmas Carol*, in time to be a Christmas book. Partly because he wanted to have *The Chimes* published so soon and partly because he wanted to hear Forster's opinion of it, partly because he was homesick for London and partly because he wanted to see a little more of Italy, Dickens decided to take a six-week trip. He would go from Genoa to England, by way of Venice. Accordingly, early in November, he and Louis Roche set out.

They boarded a stagecoach bound for the city of Piacenza. From Piacenza, they went to Modena, and from Modena to Bologna. At Bologna, they turned north and east, and after several days, got to Venice. As so many people before him had, and as so many people since, Dickens found Venice breathtaking. "The wildest visions of the Arabian Nights," he wrote to Forster, "are nothing to the Piazza of St. Mark." After Venice, he went to Verona (where Romeo and Juliet are said to have lived), and to Mantua. On November 18, he got to Milan, where he spent three days admiring the city's stupendous cathedral, and *The Last Supper* by Leonardo da Vinci. Then he

77

went north, crossed the Alps at the Simplon Pass, continued on to Basle and Strasbourg, and finally to Paris. On November 30, he was in London.

Dickens spent eight days in London. On the evening of December 3, he read *The Chimes* aloud to ten of his friends, including Forster, Thomas Carlyle, and Daniel Maclise, the painter. This public reading of something he had himself written was the first of many that Dickens was to give over the years, until his death. Everyone who ever heard him agreed that Dickens's readings were an unforgettable experience. When he read, he was an actor to the tips of his fingers. He had an endless supply of voices and accents for the different characters. His gestures and his facial expressions perfectly suited the actions and the conversations in the piece that he was reading. There is no doubt that Dickens could have been one of the great stage actors in history. Indeed, one sometimes wonders why he did not concentrate his energy on the writing of plays, with major roles in them for himself. Dickens as a playwright-actor would have met with tremendous success and applause. Shakespeare had.

Dickens's audience, on December 3, 1844, agreed that he had indeed triumphed with *The Chimes*. A great part of that particular triumph must be attributed to his powers as a reader. Although the book sold well enough when it was published, it has not managed to hold a place as one of Dickens's more popular stories.

By December 10, Dickens was back in Paris. There he watched Macready rehearsing the part of Othello. After a cold and dreary trip, he reached Marseilles, where he

boarded the steamer *Charlemagne* for Genoa. When he got
back to the Palazzo Peschiere, he noticed that the ringing
of all the bells in Genoa now seemed sweet to him. Christmas was near. His joy was capped by the arrival of a
twelfth-night cake sent to young Charley Dickens by
Angela Coutts. The cake weighed ninety pounds. Its icing
had been damaged a little in transit, and the cake had to be
sent to a baker for repairs. The baker could not resist putting it in his shopwindow for a day, after he had worked
on it. It stopped traffic. Such a cake had never been seen
before in the history of Genoa.

After the Christmas season was over, and it was time for
him to settle down to write again, Dickens found that he
was still restless. He missed his many friends—Forster and
Macready and Maclise and the others—and he missed having his house full of guests. In Genoa, he had managed to
make only a few friends that he saw gladly and regularly,
and one of these was, in a rather strange way, a "patient"
rather than a friend. Dickens had recently become interested in hypnotism and mesmerism. He had met Emile De
La Rue, a Swiss banker, and his English wife, who were
living in Genoa. It so happened that Madame De La Rue
suffered from a strange nervous, or mental, disorder. She
frequently had hallucinations and bad dreams in which
crowds of people threw stones at her, or in which a man
with an evil spirit "haunted" her. Dickens was sure that
he could cure Madame De La Rue of these hallucinations
by means of his newly acquired techniques of mesmerism.
He began to spend hours, at all times of the day and night,

trying to treat the lady. He did her some good, but his new role as healer was, understandably enough, not one that delighted Catherine.

Perhaps, then, it was partly at Catherine's urging that Dickens and his wife left Genoa for about two months, toward the end of January. They went south to Pisa, Siena, and Rome; on to Naples (where Georgina joined them, and they all climbed Mount Vesuvius) ; and then back to Rome for Holy Week.

When they got to Rome, they found that the De La Rues were there, waiting for them. Madame De La Rue had slipped downhill badly since being deprived of Dickens's mesmeric treatments. After a few days in Rome, under Dickens's care, she improved. On the Tuesday after Easter, all five of them left Rome, in one carriage, for Florence. Florence delighted Dickens: the Ponte Vecchio, the Church of Santa Croce, the great carved doors of the Cathedral Baptistry. All during the trip, Dickens continued to treat Madame De La Rue.

By April 9, they were all back in Genoa. Catherine was miserable. She was afraid that Dickens had fallen in love with his patient. Dickens protested that he was not at all in love with the lady. Catherine begged him never to see her again. Dickens insisted that he must go on with his cure, whether Catherine liked it or not. Catherine refused to have anything further to do with the De La Rues. Dickens was obliged to explain his wife's behavior as the result of a nervous breakdown.

In the middle of June, the Dickenses left Italy for good.

They crossed the Alps at the St. Gothard Pass, went north through Switzerland, and on back to England.

As he had about America, Dickens wrote a book about Italy. He called it *Pictures from Italy*. Bradbury & Evans published it. In it, Dickens did not use the bitter, critical tone that he had poured into his *American Notes*. He was a little older now, and a little wiser and more tolerant.

CHAPTER 8

Switzerland and France

In Italy, Dickens had not done much work. When he got home, he reacted to his year of idleness with a great burst of activity.

He persuaded Bradbury & Evans to start a daily newspaper, of which he would be the editor. He decided to direct, and to act in, a performance of Ben Jonson's *Every Man in His Humour*. He promised to write an article on capital punishment for the *Edinburgh Review*. He started work on a third Christmas book, *The Cricket on the Hearth*. He attacked these projects with all his usual energy and ability, but none of them turned out to be an unqualified success.

Every Man in His Humour was, of course, to be put on entirely by amateurs. Dickens took charge of everything concerned with the production, and enjoyed himself hugely. It was decided to give two performances instead of one, the second to be a charity performance for the benefit of a nursing home opposite Dickens's house in Devonshire Terrace. Celebrities crowded the theater on both evenings.

Tennyson, Lord Melbourne, the Duke of Wellington, even Prince Albert, Queen Victoria's husband, came. They watched performances by persons almost as famous as themselves: Mark Lemon and Douglas Jerrold and the artist Frank Stone, as well as Dickens, were members of the cast. Many of the comments at the end of the evening were friendly, but they seemed to have a ring of qualified praise about them—as though what was really being said was, "Not bad for amateurs." At heart, probably many of the people in the audience agreed with the remark that Lord Melbourne made, in a voice accidentally a little louder than he had intended: "I knew this play would be dull, but . . . dull as this I did not suppose."

As soon as the play was over, Dickens set to work on *The Cricket on the Hearth*. It was published in December, 1845, and was, like *A Christmas Carol* and *The Chimes*, a Christmas book. The *Times* gave it an unfavorable review, calling it "puerile and stupid." Nevertheless, it sold quite well. Today's readers may not go so far as to agree with the *Times'* first opinion; most of them do admit, however, that *The Cricket on the Hearth* is one of Dickens's dullest and weakest pieces of fiction.

While he was writing *The Cricket on the Hearth*, Dickens was also making arrangements for the launching of the newspaper. It was to be called the *Daily News*. As its editor, Dickens promptly assigned himself a salary of £2,000 a year, which was just £1,000 more than the figure that Bradbury & Evans had been thinking of. Then he started assembling a staff. A man named Powell, who had worked on both the *Morning Chronicle* and the *Evening*

Chronicle, was appointed subeditor. Douglas Jerrold and Mark Lemon agreed to do some writing. George Hogarth, Dickens's father-in-law, left the *Evening Chronicle* to become music editor.

Slightly intoxicated by this first excursion into big business, and by the huge salary that he was paying himself, Dickens invited the venerable Countess of Blessington, the good friend of Count Alfred d'Orsay, the famous dandy (as "playboys" were then being called), to contribute art news and a gossip column—and to name her own salary for doing so. Countess Blessington said that she would be glad to write for the paper, and blandly suggested that she be paid the handsome figure of £800 a year for her contributions.

Dickens was much taken aback by the amount that the countess was asking for, and he was obliged to persuade the noble lady to reduce her asking price and accept a six-month contract, at £250. As his personal secretary and assistant, Dickens named W. H. Wills, a young man who was both reliable and efficient—and so thin that Jerrold spoke of him as surely being "in training to go up a gaspipe." Dickens also found a job on the paper for his own father, who was named overseer of the staff of reporters.

The first issue of the *Daily News* appeared on January 21, 1846. Ten thousand copies were sold. (The *Times,* then the leading newspaper in London, had a circulation of twenty-five thousand.) It was, however, evidently curiosity on the part of the public that had launched the *Daily News* so well. After a few days, sales fell to about four thousand. Dickens was angry and disappointed. He had hoped that his paper would dethrone the august *Times.*

He did not know just where to place the blame for the relative failure of the enterprise. Perhaps he felt within himself that, whatever his other abilities, he did not have the particular qualifications that make a good newspaper editor. But, like many other people in similar positions, Dickens did not admit that he himself might be responsible for the paper's slender popularity and sales. He had, after all, worked hard. He did not consider that there might be a difference between working hard and working well. His anger soon settled, therefore, not on himself, but on the unfortunate Bradbury; and Bradbury joined Chapman, Hall, and Bentley on Dickens's list of hateful publishers.

William Bradbury was, undoubtedly, a bit of a fuss-budget, but undoubtedly, too, he did have something to fuss about. He and Evans had invested £22,500 in the paper. He had watched Dickens first pay himself a tremendous salary, and then offer jobs on the paper to a great number of his friends and relations. And the paper was not turning out to be a financial or journalistic success.

The inevitable happened. After seeing seventeen issues of the paper through the press, Dickens suddenly resigned as editor. Forster replaced him, but he, too, soon found Bradbury & Evans difficult to work with, and after not many months, himself resigned. After Forster, a series of other men took over the duties as editor and, in turn, quit. Clearly, the wrong had not been all on Dickens's side. The *Daily News*, however, did survive. It merged, in time, with several other newspapers, and is being published in London today as the *Daily Mail*.

Although Dickens was no longer editor of the *Daily*

News, he was still under contract to supply articles for the paper. In March, 1846, he published three pieces in it condemning public executions of criminals. He had originally promised these to the *Edinburgh Review*, but pressure of work had kept him from writing them, and the editor of the *Edinburgh Review* had excused him from his promise. Dickens's argument in his articles ran as follows: the death penalty, and particularly a public execution, acts not as a deterrent but, in fact, as an incitement to a potential murderer. A mind perverted enough to commit murder might well also be perverted enough to thrill at the possibility of paying for his deed with his life. As for public executions, nearly every criminal who himself was hanged had witnessed at least one public execution. Dickens ended by arguing for the "total abolition of the Punishment of Death." In this, he was far ahead of his times. There are still a number of countries in the world today that continue to retain a death penalty for certain crimes.

The *American Notes*, the cool reception given *Martin Chuzzlewit*, and the troubles with Chapman & Hall had, two years before, left Dickens feeling restless and upset. He had attempted to buoy up his spirits by leaving England for a year. Now, his difficulties with the *Daily News* and his quarrel with Bradbury had put him back into a restless frame of mind, and he decided again to try traveling as a remedy. On May 30, 1846, the Dickens household set out as they had before—only there were six children now: Catherine had given birth to a boy in October, 1845, and he had been baptized (not without causing considerable caustic laughter in London) Alfred d'Orsay Tennyson Dickens.

After two weeks, the Dickenses reached Lausanne, Switzerland. There they found a house (which could "have been put bodily into one of the halls" in their apartment in the Peschiere Palace) called Rosemont, which they rented for £60 for the next six months. Dickens promptly settled down to work on a new novel. It was to be called *Dombey and Son.*

For a while, Dickens was bothered by the extraordinary heat that Lausanne experienced during the summer of 1846. Then, for some inexplicable reason, Rosemont was invaded by thousands of flies. "They cover everything eatable," he wrote to Forster, "fall into everything drinkable . . . clog their legs in the lather on your chin while you are shaving. . . ." There was the temptation, too, to make a trip to Chamonix, or to spend hours in the Castle of Chillon, about which Byron had written his *Prisoner of Chillon* thirty years before. Even so, Dickens wrote on. When he had finished the first installment, he read it aloud to a group of his Lausanne acquaintances. They unanimously pronounced the work a success, and their judgment proved more right than wrong: the first part of *Dombey and Son* outsold *Chuzzlewit.* Dickens declared himself happy with the sales.

Dickens decided that it would be more pleasant to spend the winter in Paris than in Lausanne. Consequently, toward the end of November, the Dickens household ("tons of luggage . . . tons of servants . . . tons of children")

Catherine Dickens, 1846

arrived in Paris, and moved into a house on Rue de Cour-
celles in the Faubourg Saint-Honoré. Dickens, again, set
promptly to work.

He was now writing the fourth installment of *Dombey*.
In Lausanne, the heat had plagued him. In Paris, he was
bothered by the extraordinarily cold weather that the city
experienced that winter. "The water in the bed-room jugs
freezes into solid masses," he wrote in a letter to Forster
in December, "bursts the jugs . . . and rolls out on the
tables and wash-stands, hard as granite."

Even so, by Christmas, Dickens had started the fifth installment of *Dombey*, and by January 14, 1847, he had
finished it. The fifth installment contained the chapter in
which little Paul Dombey died. The death of Paul opened
the floodgates of grief that had been closed since the death of
Little Nell. Once more, the English-speaking world was
awash. Tears flowed down the unashamed cheeks of every
reader. Even Thackeray, who held a somewhat less exalted
opinion of Dickens's writings than many people, pronounced the chapter "stupendous!"

In January, Forster came over to Paris, and Dickens and
he at once set out on a series of sight-seeing tours of the
city. They went to Versailles and to the Louvre. They attended the opera and they went to the theater. Inevitably,
they met many of the famous French writers and actors of
the day, including Victor Hugo and Alexandre Dumas, two
of the few authors in the world whose popularity was to
rival Dickens's own.

Back in England, Dickens continued to work hard at
Dombey. He would write for six or eight hours each day,

and then have dinner and spend the evenings with friends and acquaintances. During June and July, he directed his company of amateur actors again. They put on *Every Man in His Humour* twice more, in Liverpool and Manchester, and earned nearly a thousand pounds for charity with their work.

Finally in March, 1848, *Dombey* was finished. Opinions differ about *Dombey and Son*. The theme of the novel is pride, and in particular, pride in having become rich and powerful through business. *Dombey* is undeniably an important novel. Professional critics and literary historians value it highly. They very much like Dickens's clear intention in the novel to try, even more vigorously than he had before, to reform the ways of the world. They think it well that Dickens could, at times, lay less emphasis on his own kind of Dickensian laughter, and become a more dedicated crusader for social and moral improvement. With the general reader, however, *Dombey and Son* is not as popular as many of Dickens's works. It seems a bit heavy, a bit melodramatic. In a word, it can be said that *Dombey* is not a lovable novel; it is an admirable one.

In February, 1849, Dickens started writing the book that was to prove his most popular, his most lovable—his most Dickensian—work. It was his own favorite among his writings. In a preface to it, he wrote: ". . . like many fond parents, I have in my heart a favorite child, and his name is David Copperfield."

To some, those sentences from the preface are very "revealing." *David Copperfield* is an autobiographical novel. Dickens stated that he preferred *Copperfield* to all his other books. That means that Dickens was interested most of all in himself. But an absorbing interest in oneself is a mark of the young; once a person becomes an adult, he is no longer so fascinated by his own thoughts and actions: he surveys with more interest society and the universe around him. By this process of reasoning, it follows that Dickens, like Peter Pan, never grew up. At his best, he remained a gifted, wonderful, and bubbling child.

Whether he ever grew up or not is, perhaps, beside the point when one reads *Copperfield*. It is not necessary to know anything about Dickens's life to appreciate the novel. And appreciate it, all but the most obstinate intellectual snobs must do. Of all of Dickens's works, this, with *Pickwick*, is the most magic.

All great writing is, among many other things, a sort of high level "con game." The author manages us, controls us, directs us. He forces us to think what we do not think when we are not reading his pages, and compels us to feel feelings that we do not ordinarily feel. There is nothing at all shameful in this, and there is much that is praiseworthy and necessary, too. Great literature exhilarates us, inspires us, raises some part of us further away from what we are, toward what we might hope, and want, to be. Few books in the world exhilarate us more than *David Copperfield*.

David is Dickens himself (David Copperfield's initials, D.C., are even Dickens's own reversed. Dickens said that he had not noticed this fact, when Forster pointed it out to him.) Mr. Micawber is Dickens's father, and Mrs. Micawber is, to a certain extent, Dickens's mother. Dora is Maria

Beadnell. Many of the things that happen to David had also happened to Dickens. It is not, however, its accuracy or truth as autobiography that makes *David Copperfield* great. What makes it great is the vigor of Dickens's creative imagination.

Other authors have written more profound books. In English, only two writers have created more vivid and lively persons and places than those that appear in *Copperfield:* they are Chaucer and Shakespeare. Mr. Micawber, the constant prodigal, takes his place beside Falstaff, and is one of the most amiable, lost black sheep ever conceived. Aunt Betsey Trotwood is a perfect portrait of a thoroughly dotty, and perfectly good-hearted, English old maiden aunt, unreal only to those persons whose experience of life is too limited to have allowed them to meet such a woman. Mr. Murdstone is the prototype of all cruel-hearted stepfathers, whether they exist as a group or not. Miss Murdstone, his sister ("She took her money out of a hard steel purse, and she kept the purse in a very jail of a bag which hung upon her arm by a heavy chain, and shut up like a bite . . ."), strikes terror into the hearts of everyone except people that honestly love machines more than they do human beings. There are Tommy Traddles and Dr. Strong and Uriah Heep and the immortal Mrs. Gummidge: "I am a lone lorn creetur'," [said Mrs. Gummidge] "and everythink goes contrairy with me."

Many of the short scenes, too, in *Copperfield* have rarely been surpassed. Chapter Five contains two of them —one in which the eight-year-old David bravely orders a meal in a restaurant, only to have it devoured by the waiter who serves it to him :

"What have we got here?" [the waiter] said, putting a fork into my dish. "Not chops?"

"Chops," I said.

"Lord bless my soul!" he exclaimed, "I didn't know they were chops . . . Ain't it lucky?"

So he took a chop by the bone in one hand, and a potato in the other, and ate away with a very good appetite, to my extreme satisfaction. He afterwards took another chop, and another potato; and after that another chop and another potato. When he had done, he brought me a pudding, and having set it before me, seemed to ruminate, and to become absent in his mind for some moments.

"How's the pie?" he said, rousing himself.

"It's a pudding," I made answer.

"Pudding!" he exclaimed. "Why bless me, so it is! What!" looking at it nearer. "You don't mean to say it's a batter-pudding?"

"Yes, it is indeed."

"Why, a batter-pudding," he said, taking up a table-spoon, "is my favourite pudding! Ain't that lucky? Come on, little 'un, and let's see who'll get most."

The waiter certainly got most. He entreated me more than once to come in and win, but what with his table-spoon to my tea-spoon, his dispatch to my dispatch, and his appetite to my appetite, I was left far behind at the first mouthful, and had no chance with him. I never saw any one enjoy a pudding so much, I think; and he laughed, when it was all gone, as if his enjoyment of it lasted still.

And that scene in which Barkis, the coachman, proposes marriage, through David, to Peggotty, David's mother's servant and housekeeper :

"So [Peggotty] makes," said Mr. Barkis, after a long interval of reflection, "all the apple parsties, and does all the cooking, do she?"

I replied that such was the fact.

"Well. I'll tell you what," said Mr. Barkis. "P'raps you might be writin' to her?"

"I shall certainly write to her," I rejoined.

"Ah!" he said, slowly turning his eyes towards me. "Well! If you was writin' to her, p'raps you'd recollect to say that Barkis was willin' : would you?"

"That Barkis was willing," I repeated, innocently. "Is that all the message?"

"Ye—es," he said, considering. "Ye—es. Barkis is willin'."

Such lines as these have the rare and touching greatness of pathos and simplicity.

This is not to say that *David Copperfield* is a faultless book. On the contrary, there are several things in it that are not only less than great, but are, in fact, real weak-

"Barkis is willin'," scene from David Copperfield

nesses. For one thing, the novel is too long, and the excuse that many Victorian novels are too long cannot undo the mischief done by the approximately two hundred excess pages. The sorrows of Little Em'ly somehow do not strike the reader as sincere or convincing; they are cut from the same cloth as the death of Little Nell and of Paul Dombey : pathetic sensationalism rather than simple pathos.

These, and a few other matters, do not essentially damage *David Copperfield*. Any man is to be estimated on his best performance, not on his worst. On the basis of *Copperfield*, Dickens confirmed his right to be thought of as one of the world's most truly great creative artists.

CHAPTER 9

Tavistock House

While he was still writing *David Copperfield*, Dickens began seriously turning over in his mind the idea of starting a weekly magazine. By New Year's Day of 1850, he had already considered and rejected several possible names for the publication. Then, he suddenly recalled the line spoken by King Henry in Shakespeare's *Henry V:* "Familiar in his mouth as household words." *Household Words* would be the magazine's name.

In spite of his *Daily News* difficulties with Bradbury & Evans, he agreed that they should be the publishers of the new magazine. Once again, Dickens started assembling an editorial staff, and once again, his father and his father-in-law were assigned places on it. Forster said that he would do some writing. The still marvelously thin Wills was made subeditor, and Dickens himself became editor (or "conductor" to use his own term) at the more modest salary this time of £500 a year.

Household Words was to concern itself with "the stirring world around us." Because of Dickens's constant interest

97

in social reform and in the championing of the downtrodden, the magazine would have a crusading flavor. Dickens wanted to use his place to campaign for such necessary social changes as prison reform, adequate city sanitation, public playgrounds for children, and safety regulations for factories. He hoped to be able to get stories or articles or poems from the leading writers of the day. In this, he was successful. A list of the various contributors to *Household Words* is virtually a list of the best-known writers then alive: Bulwer-Lytton, Charles Reade, George Meredith, Wilkie Collins, Coventry Patmore, Sheridan Le Fanu, and perhaps greatest of all, Mrs. Elizabeth Gaskell.

The first issue of *Household Words* came out at the end of March, 1850. It was a great success, and the second and third issues were equally successful. Dickens may not have been a good newspaper editor, but he quickly proved that he was a brilliant magazine editor. Dickens was probably one of the most able magazine editors that has ever lived, the equal of such different but also brilliant men as Edgar Allan Poe and Harold Ross. He managed not so much (to paraphrase George Bernard Shaw) to give his readers what they wanted, as to make his readers like what he printed for them. Nor was he unaware of his own abilities. Although Wills did a great deal of work, it was Dickens that exercised final judgment over every line that in the end was, or was not, printed. "What an amazing man!" he wrote of himself half-laughingly—and half-seriously, too —in a letter to Bradbury in March, 1850.

Although *Household Words* was primarily a reform-minded magazine, the single most famous piece published in it was a prose idyll that had no obvious crusading intentions. This was the series of sketches now known as *Cranford*, by Mrs. Gaskell. Few more exquisite pieces of prose have been written in English. Mrs. Gaskell was the beautiful wife of a wise and generous Unitarian minister of the city of Manchester. Like Dickens, she was horrified by the distressing conditions in which so many people of the time were forced to live: without decent houses, decent medical care, or decent schools. She wrote two powerful novels that attacked the social abuses of her day: *Mary Barton* and *North and South*. Like Dickens, again, she had a magnificent gift, at times, for combining sincerity with pathos, and both with lovableness. *Cranford* is her triumph in this kind, and it is written with such a tender, creative touch as

The Crown Inn. Note listing to extreme right, somewhat hidden by sign. It says "patronized by"—and the first name listed is Charles Dickens.

to deserve the name of poetry. Miss Matty, Miss Pole, Mrs. Jamieson, the cat that swallowed the lace, and the cow that was dressed in grey flannel pants to hide her hairlessness are among the most attractive inventions in all of writing.

Dickens spent a large part of the years 1851 and 1852 again at work on amateur theatricals. This time, the object of the benefit performances was an organization called the Guild of Literature and Art. The guild grew out of conversations that Dickens had with Bulwer-Lytton. Throughout history, many writers and artists had been poor and, not rarely, in bad health because they had been unable to pay for adequate medicines and medical treatment. Why should not an organization be set up that would collect money to help deserving but impoverished artists? Bulwer Lytton declared himself ready to give such an organization a piece of land that he owned, on which houses could be built and offered rent free to members of the guild. It was proposed, also, to have a fund from which men of proven artistic ability could draw a small "pension" and rising young artists might be given grants.

Dickens decided that a series of performances of plays would serve to advertise the guild, and to collect money for it. Bulwer-Lytton wrote a comedy called *Not So Bad As We Seem* for the purpose. Dickens threw himself once again into the business of directing and rehearsing the play. It was presented in London in May, and then Dickens took his company on a series of short tours. They performed, at various times, in Bristol, Manchester, Birmingham, Newcastle, Sheffield, and several other cities, and finally closed in Liverpool on September 3, 1852. They had earned £4,000 for the guild.

The theatrical tours had been a success. The guild itself, however, never did become the useful organization that Dickens and Bulwer Lytton had dreamed of. It was incorporated in 1854. The houses were built on Bulwer-Lytton's land; but the writers and artists themselves, whom the guild had been created to serve, tended to avoid it.

Just six months after Dickens had finished *Copperfield*, John Dickens died. He was sixty-six years old. If the jaunty old man had recognized himself in Mr. Micawber, he said nothing to show that he had. In any case, he would not have been offended, even though the portrait was not altogether a flattering one. He was much too good-natured for that.

Between excursions about England with his troupe of actors, Dickens kept himself hard at work on *Household Words*. He would arrive at about eight o'clock in the morning at the editorial offices, and spend most of the time that he was there, not seated at a desk, but walking back and forth in his office. While he walked, he dictated, or he simply planned and thought; frequently he would take out a pocket comb, and comb and recomb and recomb again his hair: it was a nervous habit that he had all his life.

There were now eight Dickens children. The house at Devonshire Terrace began to seem cramped and small. Dickens found a larger house in Tavistock Square, and in November, 1851, the family moved again. As soon as the last signs of moving had vanished, and everything in the house was in order, Dickens set to work on a new novel.

101

The title he gave it was *Bleak House*. He had finished the first installment by the middle of December. It came out in March of the next year, and proved to be even more of a popular success, when it appeared, than *David Copperfield*.

Catherine at this time turned to authorship, too. Under the pseudonym of Lady Maria Clutterbuck—one imagines that Dickens helped her invent that name—she published a sort of cookbook called, in a typically long nineteenth-century title, *What Shall We Have For Dinner? satisfactorily answered by numerous bills of fare for from two to eighteen persons.* Catherine had distilled into her book what she had learned through having helped to prepare literally hundreds of formal and semiformal dinners during her fifteen years of married life. Today, the stomachs of most dinner guests would boggle before one of the evening meals that Lady Clutterbuck describes. She reported a quiet dinner as having twelve courses, a formal dinner, twenty-four. Stewed kidneys would follow lobster patties, and roast lamb would follow the kidneys, and after the lamb would come the turkey and then the ham. The dinner might wind up with a plate of blancmange and cream or dressed crab or toasted cheese, or perhaps all three, one after the other. After looking over this book, one can understand why Dickens was so often short of money.

Why did Catherine turn to authorship so suddenly? It was probably in an attempt to recapture her husband's affections. There is no doubt that Dickens was gradually falling out of love with his wife. Catherine was upset by the growing estrangement. She wished that she had the verve and brilliance that would have allowed her to keep pace with Dickens, but instead, as she grew older, she became increasingly slow and clumsy. If there were a hole or a crevice anywhere, Catherine would be sure to stumble into it, and emerge with a sprained ankle or a scraped knee. At the dinner table, her bracelets would, on occasion, slide down her arms and over her hands, and land with a splash in the soup.

This physical awkwardness, which Dickens had first noticed in America, coupled with the fact that Catherine had never been exceptionally nimble intellectually, was more and more becoming a source of real annoyance to Dickens. He grew increasingly tidy and punctual and precise as he got older. He kept his own appointments to the minute, and at home he insisted that his family be all together at the table and ready to begin the meal while the clock was still striking. He not only kept his own room severely tidy, but he insisted that his children keep theirs so, too. He would not allow any of the furniture in any room in the house to be shifted so much as one inch out of the position that he had assigned to it. When he stayed at a hotel, he would often spend as much as half an hour moving the bed or the chairs or the wardrobe about, until he had found positions for them that better satisfied his taste. This kind of perfectionist behavior hardly makes for a relaxed home atmosphere; neither is it likely to improve relations between a man and his wife. Since Catherine was by nature as lethargic and easygoing as Dickens was hard-driving and precise, it was all but inevitable that in the end they would get on each other's nerves often enough to endanger their love.

103

Dickens finished *Bleak House* in August, 1853. *Bleak House* is a massive book. It is one of the three "novels of reform" that Dickens wrote in the 1850's. The chief object of Dickens's attack in *Bleak House* is (to use Hamlet's phrase in his "To be, or not to be" speech) "the law's delay."

Dickens based his story on an actual legal case. A man named Jennings had died in 1798. When he died, he left £1,500,000, but he had made no will. By 1853, the courts had not yet decided who should inherit the Jennings fortune. (Nor, it may be remarked, had the case been settled by 1915, although by then, lawyers' fees had absorbed £250,000 from the estate.) As he wrote, Dickens was thinking back to his days as a court reporter at Doctors' Commons. His own opinion of the legal profession had not changed much in twenty years. Lawyers and judges, in general, he still believed, were more interested in earning money for themselves than they were in seeing justice done.

Bleak House is not one of Dickens's more Dickensian books—as *Pickwick* and *Copperfield* and the *Christmas Carol* and *Oliver Twist* are Dickensian. It is, however, in many places a powerful book. In Chapter 8, a poor, wretched slumdweller addresses a gushing and well-intentioned but wrongheaded Lady Bountiful who comes to visit him:

". . . I wants a end of these liberties took with my place. I wants a end of being drawed like a badger. Now your're a-going to poll-pry and question according to custom—I know what you're a-going to be up to. Well! You have'nt got no occasion to be up to it. I'll save you the trouble. Is my daughter a-washin? Yes, she *is* a-washin. Look at the water. Smell it! That's wot we drinks. How do you like it, and what do you think of gin, instead! An't my place dirty? Yes, it is dirty—it's nat'rally dirty, and it's nat'rally onwholesome; and we've had five dirty and onwholesome children, as is all dead infants, and so much the better for them, and for us besides. Have I read the little book wot you left? No, I an't read the little book wot you left. There an't nobody here as knows how to read it; and if there wos, it wouldn't be suitable to me. It's a book fit for a babby, and I'm not a babby. If you was to leave me a doll, I shouldn't nuss it. How have I been conducting of myself? Why, I've been drunk for three days; and I'd a been drunk four, if I'd a had the money. Don't I never mean for to go to church? No, I don't never mean for to go to church. I shouldn't be expected there, if I did; the beadle's too gen-teel for me. And how did my wife get that black eye? Why, I giv' it her; and if she says I didn't, she's a Lie!"

And these are Dickens's words in Chapter 47, when Jo, the crossing sweeper, dies:

The light is come upon the dark benighted way. Dead!

Dead, your Majesty. Dead, my lords and gentlemen. Dead, Right Reverends and Wrong Reverends of every order. Dead, men and women, born with Heavenly compassion in your hearts. And dying thus around us every day.

Readers that prefer Dickens the Reformer to Dickens the Dickensian, will find *Bleak House* to be one of his most pleasing novels.

But even its greatest admirers admit that *Bleak House* contains a serious blemish. There is a character in it called Harold Skimpole, a silly and talkative man who is also grossly dishonest in matters of money. Mr. Micawber, in *David Copperfield*, is talkative and financially irresponsible, but Dickens painted him with love and humor. The reader laughs *with* Micawber. Skimpole is painted with anger. The reader laughs *at* him.

Harold Skimpole was based on Leigh Hunt, who was an old man but still alive when *Bleak House* came out. The reading public immediately recognized Hunt in Skimpole. Naturally, Hunt was angry to see himself so unflatteringly treated. After all, he had never offended Dickens, and he had been, when young, a social reformer nearly as vigorous as Dickens himself. It was true that Hunt was irresponsible about money, but it was largely because—and Dickens did not know this—his money was drained away by his wife, who was a secret alcoholic, and Hunt was too much of a gentleman to let his family's distress become public knowledge.

As he had been in his *American Notes*, Dickens was guilty, in *Bleak House*, of bad manners. It must be added in fairness to Dickens that several years later, having learned more about Hunt, he wrote an article apologizing publicly for Skimpole; but by then, Hunt was dead.

After he had finished *Bleak House*, Dickens decided to go to the Continent for two months. His companions were to be Augustus Egg and Egg's friend, Wilkie Collins. Collins was to become one of Dickens's closest friends over the next fifteen years, almost supplanting Forster, much to Forster's dismay. Wilkie Collins was not, at this time, an "important man" in London : he was too much the Bohemian. His dress was casual and colorful. His favorite drink was champagne. His favorite entertainment was music hall shows of a low order. He seemed always to be involved in some complicated love affair, and sometimes in two or three of them at once. He was unpunctual, untidy, lazy, kindhearted, and generous. He was also a good writer. In the course of his life, he was to turn out a number of famous novels. Poe "invented" the detective story. Collins wrote the first detective novel, and not many authors since have written more thrilling novels of suspense than Collins's *The Moonstone* and *The Woman in White*.

Collins, Egg, and Dickens left for the Continent in October, on the day after a farewell dinner given for them by Angela Coutts. First they went to Switzerland, and then south to Italy. They stopped in Milan, and then went on to Genoa. In Genoa, Dickens looked up Madame De La Rue. Her dreams and hallucinations were not bothering her so much any more, she said, and she refused Dickens's offer to give her a few final mesmeric treatments. Dickens wrote Catherine about his having seen the De La Rues, and Catherine, perhaps under a little pressure from her husband, so far conquered her jealousy as to write a friendly note to Madame De La Rue.

From Genoa, the three travelers took a steamer to Naples. Inevitably, the energetic Dickens compelled his two friends to climb Mount Vesuvius. From Naples, they went to Rome, and then north through Siena and Florence to Venice. From Venice, they started home. Dickens was back in Tavistock House by December 11.

Just after Christmas, in the city of Birmingham, Dickens gave his first public reading of passages from his own books. He had always been interested in the theater and in acting; he had already often read aloud things that he had written, but so far only to small circles of friends and acquaintances. Now, for the first time, he read aloud to a paying audience. More than two thousand people came to the Birmingham Town Hall to listen as he read from the *Christmas Carol* and *The Cricket on the Hearth*. The readings were an enormous success. The applause was deafening. He did not know it, of course, but there in the Birmingham Town Hall, during the Christmas season of 1853, Dickens was entering upon a second career that was to make him even more famous and more beloved than he already was. That career was also to ruin his health and to hurry him to his premature death.

The circulation of *Household Words* was beginning now, for imponderable reasons, to slide slowly downhill. Dickens decided to try to remedy matters by writing a novel that he would publish in the magazine in serial form. He called the novel *Hard Times*. It appeared between April and August, 1854, and it succeeded in more than doubling the circulation of the magazine. In order to be able to finish writing the book in relative peace and quiet, Dickens crossed the Channel and rented a house for the summer at Boulogne. There, characteristically, he "moved every article of furniture in the house" before he could settle down to work.

Hard Times is the least Dickensian and the most reform-minded of all of Dickens's novels. Its theme is the moral, mental, and physical discomfort caused by the new factories and recent industrialization of England, and by the badly administered divorce laws. *Hard Times* is shorter than most of Dickens's novels. There is not much humor and fun in it. It is written in crisper language than Dickens usually used. The credibility of the story is, perhaps,

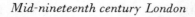

Mid-nineteenth century London

stretched a little, because the good characters seem a bit
too good and the villains seem a bit too black. In *Hard
Times*, Dickens was fixing his attention on situations and
on groups, more than he was on individuals. Some people
(George Bernard Shaw was among them) have felt that
Hard Times was perhaps Dickens's greatest novel; others
have gone so far as to call it "Dickens's most conspicuous
failure."

In *Bleak House* and *Hard Times* (and in *Little Dorritt*, his
next novel), Dickens was by no means campaigning for
reforms that were not needed, nor angrily attacking evils
that did not exist. On the contrary, social conditions in
England during the 1850's were very bad indeed.

By 1851, half of the population of England was living
in the cities, and the cities were overcrowded, dangerous,
and filthy. Vermin, maggots, mice, and rats were everywhere. Fresh water was a rarity, and municipal plumbing
was so primitive that sewage regularly seeped into what
fresh water pipes there were. Outbreaks of cholera (a painful disease that attacks the stomach and intestines), brought
on largely by bad sanitation, killed from fifteen to thirty
thousand people each year. Frequently, there were long
waits before the services of undertakers and graveyards
became available. On occasion, corpses had to be kept for
days in a house, or thrown surreptitiously into the public
streets, where they lay in the gutters until the stench set up
by their decomposition caused the offended citizens to pitch
them, by night, into a nearby river or canal. The food
available to the poor was, on the whole, what can be de-

scribed only as garbage. Children, as soon as they could walk, were sent out to forage for scraps, or were put to work as riverbank scavengers ("mud larks"), chimney sweeps, crossing sweepers, or stable boys. Few children ever had any schooling. Fewer still owned any toys or playthings. Not rarely, children playing ball in the streets used, instead of a ball, the body of a dead kitten.

At this time, when there was so much work to be done at home, England allowed herself to be drawn into war. (History shows that nations often get involved in foreign wars when difficulties at home become serious.) Between 1854 and 1856, England fought on the side of Turkey against Russia, in a conflict called the Crimean War. Today, the Crimean War is remembered chiefly for two things: the Battle of Balaclava, in October, 1854, in which took place the famous Charge of the Light Brigade; and the work of Florence Nightingale who, almost single-handed, founded the profession of hospital nursing as we know it today. In 1854, Florence Nightingale went to work in the British military hospital at Scutari in Turkey. The conditions at that hospital, which had been set up to care for the soldiers who had been wounded in battle in the service of their country, were brutal and chaotic to a degree that baffles the understanding. Lytton Strachey, in his *Eminent Victorians*, has described what the thirty-four-year-old Miss Nightingale found upon her arrival at Scutari:

The very building itself was radically defective. Huge sewers underlay it, and cesspools loaded with filth wafted their poison into the upper rooms. The

111

floors were in so rotten a condition that many of them could not be scrubbed; the walls were thick with dirt; incredible multitudes of vermin swarmed everywhere. And, enormous as the building was, it was yet too small. It contained four miles of beds, crushed together so close that there was but just room to pass between them. Under such conditions, the most elaborate system of ventilation might well have been at fault; but here there was no ventilation. The stench was indescribable. . . . The structural defects were equalled by the deficiencies in the commonest objects of hospital use. There were not enough bedsteads; the sheets were of canvas, and so coarse that the wounded men recoiled from them, begging to be left in their blankets; there was no bedroom furniture of any kind, and empty beer bottles were used for candlesticks. There were no basins, no towels, no soap, no brooms, no mops, no trays, no plates; there were neither slippers nor scissors, neither shoe-brushes nor blacking; there were no knives or forks or spoons. The supply of fuel was constantly deficient. The cooking arrangements were pre-posterously inadequate, and the laundry was a farce. As for purely medical materials, the tale was no better. Stretchers, splints, bandages—all were lacking; and so were the most ordinary drugs.

Nor were many of the public hospitals in the England of the time much cleaner or much more efficient than that English military pesthole on the Bosporus, in Asia. Florence Nightingale, when she returned home, worked ceaselessly toward making hospitals the clean, quiet, reliable institutions that so many of them are today. "She spent her life, one might say, in displacing and defeating Mrs. Gamp."

Yet, in spite of all the filth and poverty and needless cruelty in England at this time, the government, in 1860, spent £26,000,000 on defense and the military, and just £15,000,000 on problems and conditions at home. Small wonder that Dickens was angry.

CHAPTER 10
Gad's Hill

About thirty miles east of London lies the cathedral city of Rochester. Two miles from Rochester, there is a small hill known as Gad's Hill. Shakespeare used Gad's Hill as the setting for one of his most famous scenes. It is there, in *Henry IV*, *Part One*, that Sir John Falstaff robs a party of travelers and is immediately set upon by his friend Hal, the Prince of Wales (in disguise), and robbed of his robbings.

In Dickens's day, there was a handsome house on Gad's Hill. It was built of brick, covered with ivy, and flanked by cedars; and it had a large garden. Dickens had seen this house many times. When he was a boy, living in Chatham, he and his father had gone on walks that had taken them past Gad's Hill Place (as the house was called). John Dickens had laughingly said to Charles that if he worked hard, he might one day live there.

On March 14, 1856, Dickens became the owner of Gad's Hill Place.

For the last year or so, Dickens had been at work on a new novel that he finally decided to call *Little Dorrit* in-

stead of *Nobody's Fault*. He was finding the novel difficult
to write. He spent the summer of 1856 at Boulogne. Several more things had happened that had put him rather out
of sorts. Forster, partly because he was jealous of Dickens's
growing friendship with Wilkie Collins, had huffily decided
to give up writing for *Household Words*. Macready had
come to see Dickens in Paris. He had retired from the stage.
Although Macready was only sixty-three years old,
Dickens was saddened to see that his old friend was pre-
maturely aged and almost failing. Catherine's parents, too,
were beginning to get on his nerves. They were taking ad-
vantage, he thought, of the fact that he had more money
than they had. They felt no embarrassment about turning
over to him, now and then, a few bills to pay, or suggesting
to him that they move into Tavistock House whenever he
was away.

By June 1, 1857, the Dickenses were settled in Gad's
Hill Place. They now had two houses, since they had not
given up Tavistock House. Their first houseguest was due
in a few days: Hans Christian Andersen, the Danish writer,
who is famous today chiefly for his brilliant fables and
fairy tales such as *The Ugly Duckling* and *The Emperor's
New Clothes*. He arrived on June 8. After he had been at
Gad's Hill for only a little while, Dickens began to believe
that Andersen was himself something of an ugly duckling.
He was just the type of man that Dickens did not like. He
was timid, nervous, and sensitive. He spoke English,
French, Italian, and German in such a way that Dickens
could understand little of what he said. Every once in a
while, for no apparent reason, he would suddenly burst

into tears. His chief pastime, while he stayed with the Dickenses, was to cut pieces of paper into endless varieties of lace and little human figures, and to weave complex chains and crowns of wild flowers. Catherine liked Andersen, and warmed to his shy, childlike ways, and so did Angela Coutts when she met him. Dickens did not.

Andersen had been invited to stay for two weeks. When the two weeks were over, Dickens, purely formally, urged him to stay on. Andersen took him by surprise by thanking him and agreeing to remain. Finally, after five weeks altogether with the Dickenses, he left. He burst into tears as he boarded the train. He had been the guest, he sobbed, of the greatest writer in the world. Dickens put a card on the mirror in the room that Andersen had occupied : "Hans Christian Andersen slept in this room for five weeks— which seemed to the family *ages!*"

On June 8, 1857, Dickens's friend Douglas Jerrold died suddenly. Dickens immediately decided that something must be done for Jerrold's widow and children. Jerrold had not been able to leave much money. A fund must be raised. Wilkie Collins had recently written a play called *The Frozen Deep*. Dickens had already directed several amateur performances of it, and they had been a success The play would be put on again. Admission would be charged, and the proceeds would be turned over to Mrs. Jerrold.

The performances were duly given. The play was again a great success. Queen Victoria herself came one evening to see it. Dickens was invited to take his cast to the city of Manchester, and put the play on there. The excitement of

producing a play, and the resounding applause of the
crowds, were successful once more in stirring Dickens, for
a while, out of a mood of depression. There was only one
unpleasant note. Jerrold's son pointed out several times
to his friends that, on the contrary, the family had not
been left in poverty, and he rather resented Dickens's publicly "passing the hat around" for their benefit.

The last installment of *Little Dorrit* appeared in June,
1857. The novel had been popular with the public. The
average English reader's tastes had changed since 1837.
When Dickens had first started to write, nostalgia and
kindly laughter and innocent virtue maltreated were the
things the public wanted. Such lessons as Dickens had
"taught" in *Oliver Twist* and *Nicholas Nickleby* had had
to be well disguised with comedy and a certain amount of
factual improbability. By the 1850's, both Dickens's ap-
proach and the public taste had altered. The social problems
that England was facing now seemed too serious. One could
no longer laugh. In *Bleak House* and in *Hard Times*, and
again in *Little Dorrit*, Dickens behaved toward England as
he had behaved in *Martin Chuzzlewit* toward America. Instead of writing chiefly about individuals, he considered,
and indicted, his entire country. The public liked the new
technique. *Little Dorrit* sold very well. Only a few readers
regretted what seemed to be the silencing of Dickens's
Dickensian ability: the ability that had produced Mr. Pickwick and Mr. Bumble and Mr. Pecksniff and Mr. Micawber. Thackeray was among them. He said that *Little Dorrit*
was "dead stupid."

The theme of *Little Dorrit* is that society is a restraining force, the world is a prison, and all men are confined, restricted, brutalized prisoners within it. The idea that man is a prisoner, that he can rarely do what he wants to do, that he has been hobbled and changed for the worse by laws and taboos and prohibitions, that perhaps men's bodies themselves are chiefly prison houses confining men's hearts and souls—such ideas as these had been expressed by many writers before Dickens. There was Shakespeare:

> *Hamlet.* ... what have you, my good friends, deserved at the hands of Fortune, that she sends you to prison hither?
>
> *Guildenstern.* Prison, my lord!
>
> *Hamlet.* Denmark's a prison.
>
> *Rosencrantz.* Then is the world one.
>
> *Hamlet.* A goodly one; in which there are many confines, wards, and dungeons, Denmark being one o' the worst.
>
> *Rosencrantz.* We think not so, my lord.
>
> *Hamlet.* Why then, 'tis none to you; for there is nothing either good or bad, but thinking makes it so: to me it is a prison.

(*Hamlet:* II, ii)

and there was Matthew Arnold, who wrote, in *A Summer Night*, in 1852:

> For most men in a brazen prison live,
> Where, in the sun's hot eye

118

With heads bent o'er their toil, they languidly
Their lives to some unmeaning taskwork give,
Dreaming of nought beyond their prison-wall . . .
Death in their prison reaches them,
Unfreed, having seen nothing, still unblest.

Prisons had always interested Dickens : they appear in
many of his writings. One of the early *Sketches by Boz* was
A Visit to Newgate. In *Pickwick*, prison has a prominent
role, and so it has in *David Copperfield* and *A Tale of Two
Cities*, as well as in *Little Dorrit*. Doubtless, Dickens had
this interest in prisons partly because his own father had
been put into Marshalsea Prison for debt.

At this time, while he was writing about imprisonment
and confinement and restriction, Dickens was himself becoming more and more restless at home. He was beginning
to feel that marriage itself was a sort of prison. The fact
was that he was simply no longer in love with Catherine.
Everything that she did and did not do now annoyed him.
He began to wish strongly that he were unmarried again,
free and unattached. During the whole course of his life,
what Dickens really wanted, he usually managed somehow
to get.

The story of Dickens's separation from his wife is not
a pleasant one. It began, in earnest, in Manchester, in August, 1857. Dickens had made plans to have *The Frozen
Deep* performed there on behalf of the Jerrold Fund. The
theater that the group was to use was a large one, called
the Free Trade Hall. Because the theater was so big, Dickens

Charles Dickens and his dogs

was afraid that his two daughters and the other ladies in the original cast, none of whom were professional actresses, would not be able to make themselves heard in it. He, therefore, asked a well-known actress, Mrs. Frances Ternan, and two of her daughters, Maria and Ellen, also professional actresses, to be in the Manchester performances. They agreed. It turned out that *The Frozen Deep* had never been done better than it was in Manchester. Dickens himself acted supremely well. According to Collins, "he electrified the audience."

Collins did not say it, but Dickens had himself been electrified too—by Ellen Ternan. She was eighteen years old, small, blonde, and pretty. It is hardly surprising, therefore, even if it is a little sad, to find these lines in a letter that Dickens wrote to Forster in September, 1857, after the Manchester performances: "Poor Catherine and I are not made for each other, and there is no help for it. It is not only that she makes me uneasy and unhappy, but that I make her so too . . ." Nor did Dickens confine his complaints about his homelife to the ears of his closest friends. In October, 1857, he wrote to Madame De La Rue that he was not "getting on well" with "a certain poor lady you know of . . ." "Neither do the children," he added. He seemed to be trying to justify, in advance, what he had already made up his mind he would do.

For a time, Dickens was kept from separating openly from his wife, partly by professional considerations. In the public view, he was a moral writer, one who had long celebrated the joys of happy married life. What would happen to his popularity and to his reputation if his own marriage were to break up? What would happen to his income? How would he be able to support his nine children?

Inevitably, something happened to override these considerations and to confirm Dickens in his determination that he and his wife must part. He bought a bracelet for Ellen Ternan. The jeweler, by mistake, sent the bracelet to Catherine. Understandably, Catherine was furious. Dickens protested that his friendship with Ellen was purely formal and innocent. Catherine poured out her anguish into the ears of her parents. They advised her to leave Dickens.

It was finally decided, in May, 1858, that Catherine would move into a house of her own, and that Dickens would allow her £600 a year. It was also decided that Georgina, strangely enough, would not leave with her. She had regularly taken Dickens's part against Catherine in family disagreements. Now she declared that she would stay with Dickens, and continue to run his house and look after the children.

Suddenly, something else happened, and "my father," Dickens's daughter Kate said, "was like a madman." Dickens heard that Mrs. Hogarth and Catherine's sister, Helen, were telling to anyone that cared to listen that Dickens's friendship with Ellen Ternan was not quite as formal and innocent as Dickens had declared it to be. With the snarl of rage typical of either an innocent man wrongly accused, or of a guilty man caught in the act—there is no evidence to show which of the two Dickens at that moment was—Dickens unleashed all the anger and annoyance with

Catherine and the Hogarth family that he had had pent up for years.

First, he retracted Catherine's £600 allowance until Mrs. Hogarth and Helen had signed a humiliating statement to the effect that they were sure that Dickens and Ellen Ternan were nothing more than the most innocent of friends. Then, in a paroxysm of rage and anguish, he determined to publish a statement that he and Ellen were not involved in any scandalous relationship. He ranged the streets of London from one publisher's office to another, in search of support and advice. John Delane, the editor of the *Times*, said that he thought that such a statement would be a good idea. Mark Lemon, however, refused to print it in *Punch*, and for this Dickens severed their friendship of many years' standing. Bradbury and Evans tried to persuade Dickens not to use the pages of *Household Words* as an airing place for his family quarrels, but Dickens would not listen. On June 12, 1858, readers of his magazine were somewhat startled to see the following:

> Some domestic trouble of mine, of long-standing
> . . . has been made the occasion of misrepresenta-
> tions, most grossly false, most monstrous, and most
> cruel—involving, not only me, but innocent persons
> dear to my heart . . . I most solemnly declare . . .
> that all the . . . rumours . . . are abominably
> false. And that whosoever repeats one of them after
> this denial, will lie as wilfully and as foully as it is
> possible . . . to lie . . .

123

At the same time, Dickens wrote a second, more vigorous and explicit statement on this same subject, which he intended to publish only if his first declaration did not scotch the rumors:

Two wicked persons, who should have spoken very differently of me . . . have . . . coupled with this separation the name of a young lady for whom I have a great attachment and regard. I will not repeat her name—I honour it too much. Upon my soul and honour, there is not on this earth a more virtuous and spotless creature than that young lady. I know her to be as innocent and pure, and as good as my own dear daughters. Further, I am quite sure that Mrs. Dickens, having received this assurance from me, must now believe it, in the respect I know her to have for me, and in the perfect confidence I know her in her better moments to repose in my truthfulness.

These bitter words, too, found their way into print in both England and the United States, though probably without Dickens's consent. A few papers and magazines now editorialized harshly, not on the fact that Dickens and his wife had separated, but on Dickens's "selfishness and heartlessness" in having tattled all his private grievances to the reading public. Catherine, for her part, living meekly in her new house apart from her husband, gave no statements to the press, and added no more fuel to the fire of her husband's rage.

Gradually, Dickens calmed down again. He had alienated the whole Hogarth family, except Georgina. He had made himself for a time the subject of rumor and gossip throughout the English-speaking world. He had muddied, however unintentionally, Ellen Ternan's name. But he was free of his listless, awkward, stumbling wife.

Dickens spent the summer and fall of 1858, after the final breakup of his marriage, on a tour of England, Scotland, and Ireland, giving public readings from his books. He presented himself in over a hundred cities and towns. It was as though he were challenging the public to disapprove of him for having separated so publicly from Catherine. He gave them the chance to disapprove; but he really wanted, and really needed, demonstrations of the public's continuing respect and affection. All his life, off and on, he had been at odds with his friends and his family. His father and mother had hurt him by putting him to work in the blacking factory. Maria Beadnell had rejected his love. Bentley, Chapman and Hall, and Bradbury and Evans had (he felt) dealt with him unfairly. John Forster was not the warm friend now that he once had been. His friendship with Mark Lemon was no more. (Only after nearly ten years were Dickens and Lemon reconciled.) Even Angela Coutts had shown sympathy for Catherine during the separation arrangements. Dickens had never been able to get along warmly and serenely with the people that he knew, even with the people that he loved, and that loved him, the most.

But what of the public—the great, anonymous public? For them (as well as because of an inner compulsion), he had done his writing. He had always tried hard to amuse them, to entertain them, to be their champion. He had given them great presents of laughter and of tears. He had unfailingly used his inextinguishable energy to take the part of the weak and the sick and the old and the helpless among them. Would they, too, abandon him, withdraw their affection simply because he had left his wife?

A few days after he had published his "domestic trouble" statement in *Household Words*, Dickens was scheduled to give a public reading in St. Martin's Hall, in London. He walked out onto the stage stiffly, slowly, almost aggressively. If he was nervous, he gave no sign of it. He went to the reading desk at the center of the stage, and turned and faced the audience.

A tumult of applause swept through the theater. The crowd rose to their feet, clapping and waving and cheering. The roar of respect and affection that they sent up might have been heard, it is said, half a mile away. Whatever Dickens the man had done, Dickens the writer was secure in the hearts of the public.

The whole five-month tour was a triumph. Dickens read superbly well. He flashed miraculously from one character to another, becoming completely each of them in turn. When he read Mrs. Gamp, he *was* Mrs. Gamp, "snuffy, husky, and unctuous" and fat. When he read Paul Dombey, he *was* little Paul Dombey, dying right there before the audience's eyes. Everywhere he went, the cheers and the applause were deafening. Over and over again, people stopped him on the street in every city he went to: "God bless you, Mr. Dickens, for the light you have been in my house this many a year." Never has any writer in history been so affectionately acclaimed.

The tour ended in November, 1858. Dickens was exhilarated by the reception he had had. He was not so exhilarated, however, that he had forgotten the fact that Bradbury & Evans had strongly urged him, a few months before, to keep his marital troubles out of *Household Words*. This had been betrayal. Dickens decided to sever all relations with them. Once again, he would change publishers. He rapidly made arrangements to go back to Chapman & Hall. William Hall had been dead now for ten years. Edward Chapman was about to retire and turn the management of the business over to his cousin Frederic Chapman. The bitter things that had been said over *Chuzzlewit* were forgotten. Chapman & Hall would be glad to become Dickens's publishers once more.

There remained the problem of *Household Words*. Bradbury & Evans had a considerable financial interest in it. The magazine was doing well. They did not want to lose a sure source of income. But there was little that they could do. Dickens resigned as "conductor" of *Household Words* on May 28, 1859. With Chapman & Hall, he quickly founded a new magazine of exactly the type of *Household Words*, and called it *All the Year Round*. Bradbury & Evans responded by bringing out a rival to it that they called *Once a Week*.

Once a Week managed to be moderately successful. *All the Year Round* was an enormous success. Even with Dickens as conductor, *Household Words* had never had a circulation of more than about fifty thousand—which was a very high figure in the 1850's. *All the Year Round*, after a few years, sold as many as three hundred thousand copies a week.

His confidence in himself restored by the success of the reading tour, Dickens decided to write a new novel with which to launch his new magazine. The first installment appeared in the first issue. The novel proved to be, taken all in all, one of his best and most enduring works. It was *A Tale of Two Cities*.

With the first few pages of *A Tale of Two Cities*, it was immediately clear to Dickens, and clear to his public, that neither his family difficulties nor his new second career as a public reader had diminished his powers as a writer. They seemed, indeed, to have increased them. The second chapter of *A Tale of Two Cities*, telling of the delivery of the mysterious message to Jarvis Lorry, while the Dover Mail is lumbering through the mud and mist up Shooter's Hill, is one of the most forceful pieces of descriptive writing that Dickens ever did.

A Tale of Two Cities is altogether a moving and a powerful book. Not strangely, since Dickens's whole life had changed just before he wrote it, it is different in many ways from his earlier books. It is a historical novel, set in the days of the French Revolution. It contains only a few moments of Dickensian whimsy and fun, and they are, for the most part, concentrated in Jeremy Cruncher and his wife and son. It contains moments of pathos that are far more moving than the deaths of Little Nell and Paul Dombey. Oscar Wilde once said—and he was not entirely wrong

—that a man must have a heart of stone if he can read about the death of Little Nell without laughing. He could not have said, and did not say, the same of *A Tale of Two Cities*. There are few people that read the death of Sydney Carton without being profoundly moved.

Sydney Carton is a lawyer, about thirty years old when the book opens. He is lazy, and he drinks too much. He seems to be unable to pull himself together. He loves Lucie Manette, but she cannot love him; and she marries Charles Darnay Evrémonde. Darnay Evrémonde is arrested and sentenced to death during the Reign of Terror. He has done nothing himself to deserve death. Carton bribes his way into Darnay's cell. He drugs Darnay, changes clothes with him, and has him carried out of the prison, back to Lucie, free and safe. He has decided that he will go to the guillotine in Darnay's place. It is the morning of the execution. Fifty-two persons have been sentenced to die that day. They are led into a large, dark room to wait:

As [Carton] stood by the wall in a dim corner, while some of the fifty-two were brought in after him, one man stopped in passing, to embrace him, as having a knowledge of him. It thrilled him with a great dread of discovery; but the man went on. A very few moments after that, a young woman, with a slight girlish form, a sweet spare face in which there was no vestige of colour, and large widely opened patient eyes, rose from the seat where he had observed her sitting, and came to speak to him.

"Citizen Evrémonde," she said, touching him with her cold hand. "I am a poor little seamstress, who was with you in La Force."

He murmured for answer: "True. I forget what you were accused of?"

"Plots. Though the just Heaven knows I am innocent of any. Is it likely? Who would think of plotting with a poor little weak creature like me?"

The forlorn smile with which she said it, so touched him, that tears started from his eyes.

"I am not afraid to die, Citizen Evrémonde, but I have done nothing. I am not unwilling to die, if the Republic which is to do so much good to us poor, will profit by my death; but I do not know how that can be, Citizen Evrémonde. Such a poor weak little creature!"

As the last thing on earth that his heart was to warm and soften to, it warmed and softened to this pitiable girl.

"I heard you were released, Citizen Evrémonde. I hoped it was true."

"It was. But, I was again taken and condemned."

"If I may ride with you, Citizen Evrémonde, will you let me hold your hand? I am not afraid, but I am little and weak, and it will give me more courage."

As the patient eyes were lifted to his face, he saw a sudden doubt in them, and then astonishment. He pressed the work-worn, hunger-worn young fingers, and touched his lips.

"Are you dying for him?" she whispered.

Sydney Carton going to his death in A Tale of Two Cities

"And his wife and child. Hush! Yes."

"Oh, you will let me hold your brave hand, stranger?"

"Hush! Yes, my poor sister; to the last."

And the novel ends with a sentence that has become one of the most famous in the English language:

"It is a far, far better thing that I do, than I have ever done; it is a far, far better rest that I go to, than I have ever known."

Although *A Tale of Two Cities* is different from most of Dickens's novels in many ways, it is similar to them in some. *Two Cities* is, like much of Dickens's writing, largely autobiographical and reminiscent. It is, however, a more subtle book in this vein than many that had preceded it. The memories and the events of Dickens's life are buried more deeply in it, and he managed to turn them into more valid drama than he had usually been capable of.

Lucie Manette is clearly Ellen Ternan: young, blonde, pretty, and affectionate. Dickens himself is both Charles Darnay, who loves Lucie but almost loses her forever, and Sydney Carton, who would do anything at all to give her happiness. The bitter, hysterical mobs in Paris during the Reign of Terror, and in London during the spy trials, are the crowds that Dickens had watched as they gloated and howled at the public hanging, years before, of François Courvoisier.

In *A Tale of Two Cities*, Dickens seems to have reached

(perhaps to have returned to) the conviction that a high moral level will be reached by society only when each single man in society leads a highly moral life. No society can be any better, nor any worse, than the single persons that make it up. In the swirl and turmoil of the warring revolutionary factions in the novel, it is one man that commands our attention and respect. He is what is rare, a man not moved at all by self-interest, but purely by his love for another person. A terrible opportunity is given him, and from somewhere he finds the personal courage not to shrink from it. "The little, nameless, unremembered acts" become in him "the great and gallant long-remembered act of bravery and of love—that best portion of a good man's life."

A Tale of Two Cities is a relatively short novel. The action moves swiftly. Many of the characters have profited by Dickens's speed and conciseness—Sydney Carton, above all. Carton is one of Dickens's most appealing characters. He is languid, lazy, intelligent, and self-effacing, possessed of tenderness and wit and grace. Like Dickens, the creative artist, he was willing to go to any lengths at all to offer help to a person that he loved. And Carton may well have been given the serene and noble character that Dickens the man secretly wished that he himself possessed, but knew he never could.

CHAPTER 11

America Once More

If not like Sydney Carton, what was Dickens the man like at this time in his life? In 1860, he was forty-eight years old. His hair was grey (but he touched it up a little now and then to keep it from looking too grey). He had a beard and a moustache. His eyes were dark. His glance was intense, and when he looked directly at you, it was almost hypnotic. His forehead was broad and high. He was still possessed of wonderful physical vigor. He thought nothing of taking a ten- or twelve-mile walk daily, going every step of the way at a speed of at least four miles an hour. These walks became famous. Many weekend guests at Gad's Hill learned to dread them. Dickens, swinging a blackthorn walking stick, would stride on, seemingly growing stronger and stonger as the miles went by, talking and laughing, and once in a while chaffing those of his companions who were sweating and weary and starting to lag behind after an hour or two. "Dickens, the Relentless Pedestrian," was the subject of a number of private jokes, and at least one newspaper cartoon of the day.

He disliked London now. It had become a "vile place" to him, and he wondered "what on earth I do there except of obligation." In order to cut one more tie with the city, and with his past life, he planned to sell Tavistock House and spend all of his time, when he was not traveling, at Gad's Hill. Forster, ever conscious of social values, tried to advise him not to get rid of the old house. Dickens's daughters, he argued, would be lonely in the country, and anyway, Dickens ought to have a city house in which to entertain the important people of London. Dickens disregarded the advice, sold Tavistock House to a banker named Davis, and only compromised so far as to agree to rent a furnished house in town for a month or two in the winter.

Dickens's children were doing well, now, but not brilliantly. Young Charley was trying his hand at the tea business, and in 1860, he went to China on a buying trip. Walter joined the armed forces, went to India, and was promoted to lieutenant before he was eighteen. Frank was afflicted with a bad stammer. Dickens found a place for him, early in 1861, on *All the Year Round*, but he did not do very well at the job. After two years he, too, went to India, where he joined the Bengal Mounted Police. Alfred, in 1860, was planning to become an army engineer. Sydney, in the same year, although he was only twelve, was determined that he would join the navy. Harry and Edward (who was nicknamed "Plorn") were both students at the Rochester Grammar School.

Dickens's two daughters were quite different from each other in character. Mary was mild and quiet. She had taken her father's side at the time of the separation, and she refused to see her mother again as long as Dickens was alive. Kate was hot-tempered and stubborn. She had not approved of the separation, and she had several dark things to say about Georgina, and about life at home as Dickens's daughter. In 1860, she accepted a proposal from Charles Collins, Wilkie Collins's brother. Predictably, Dickens did not approve of the match, and tried to argue Kate out of it. He failed. Kate was married on July 17. Catherine did not attend the wedding.

Dickens, at the age of forty-eight, was world famous, rich, and in good health. He was, as his recent reading tour had shown him, one of the most respected and beloved men alive. He seemed to have lost none of his ability as a writer. He was what he had said that he wanted to be—separated from his wife. As the world judges of these matters, Dickens was an extraordinarily successful man. He ought, by all rights, to have been happy.

He was not happy. All his life, from time to time, he had fallen prey to moods of restlessness and uneasiness. He had usually tried to settle his spirits by traveling or by working harder or by finding even more things to do: plays to produce, speeches to give, dinners to attend. He had, as it were, tried to repair the sputtering machinery by moving it from place to place. Now, instead of growing calmer in middle age, he grew still more active and energetic. It was as if he were being pursued by some demon. He was not content simply to *be* a writer—and a great one. He must be *doing* something—anything. He himself recognized that he was being driven on by some nameless, unseen force. He even regretted being the whirlwind of energy that he knew that he was. Sometimes he was afraid that his writing would suffer as a result of his personal vigor. "I have as great a delight in [my writing] as the most enthusiastic of my readers," he told Angela Coutts, "and the sense of my trust and responsibility . . . is always upon me. If *I* were soured, I should still try to sweeten the lives and fancies of others . . ." But he also had to admit that he was often so restless, so nervous, so pushed, that "the scaling of all the Mountains in Switzerland . . . would be but slight relief."

Whatever Dickens's demon was, it was to drive him to his death within ten years.

The second novel that was serialized in *All the Year Round* was Wilkie Collins's *The Woman in White*. The public liked it. The third one was called *A Day's Ride*. It was by an Irish novelist, then of considerable reputation, named Charles Lever. Dickens had enjoyed the first two or three installments of Lever's work. They were, he said, full of vivacity and originality. The public did not agree with him. They were bored by Lever's story, and many of them gave up buying *All the Year Round*. Its circulation began to "drop rapidly and continuously."

There was only one thing to do: publish a new novel by Dickens himself in the magazine. Dickens started work at once. On December 1, 1860, there appeared the first installment of *Great Expectations*.

Great Expectations is, after *David Copperfield*, Dickens's most thoroughly autobiographical novel. He recognized that in his haste to get a novel ready he was running the risk of repeating himself. He guarded against this by re-reading *Copperfield*—and was "affected by it," he said, "to a degree you would hardly believe." He did not, in the end, repeat himself at all.

Dickens, who was David in *David Copperfield*, is Pip in *Great Expectations*. Instead of making himself an orphan after a few chapters, as he had David, he made himself an orphan before the book opens. (Because of his parents' nearly total lack of any sense of domestic responsibility, Dickens had always felt that he had really never had any parents, as parents are generally thought of.) Instead of being put to work in a blacking factory, Pip is apprenticed to his brother-in-law, Joe Gargery, who is a blacksmith. Instead of owing the upturn in his life to his father's release from prison, Pip owes his to the escape from prison, and sudden prosperity in Australia (where Dickens had finally dispatched Mr. Micawber), of a convict named Magwitch.

Abel Magwitch makes a fortune, and decides to spend it all on making Pip into a gentleman. Pip has no idea who his benefactor is. He rather thinks that it is mad Miss Havisham, the guardian of the cold, beautiful, bewitching Estella. He goes to London, lives well, studies, and does his best to forget his humble youth in the blacksmith shop. Magwitch reappears illegally in England, is captured, and dies. His vast fortune is forfeit to the government. Pip is left with nothing. Estella has married another. Pip starts out to make his own way in the world.

There the novel ought to have ended. Pip's great expectations were to have been expectations only. At this point, Bulwer Lytton intervened. He persuaded Dickens to add a chapter in which, through a further turn of circumstance, Pip and Estella could be married. Such an ending may have gone against Dickens's artistic sensibilities. It did not altogether displease his feelings as a man. Estella is in part Maria Beadnell, and partly Ellen Ternan, too.

It is clear in *Great Expectations*, as it was in *Two Cities*, that no matter what the nature of the demon that was driving him, Dickens had not lost his literary genius. The opening chapter of the book, in which Pip as a boy first meets the escaped Magwitch in the graveyard near the marsh, is done with all of Dickens's old power to blend into one what is terrifying and what is funny. The atmosphere of some of the scenes in Miss Havisham's decaying house are unforgettable. Mr. Wemmick's Aged Parent—"Aged P"—is one of Dickens's most brilliant minor characters.

It was as a rapid writer, as a writer able to produce short, sharp, clear scenes, that Dickens had always done his best work. He was at his greatest when he was at his most spontaneous. When he slowed down to think, to plan, to build a plot, his writing suffered. Nowhere is this more true and evident than in *Great Expectations*.

Dickens the creator can manage us. We do not notice— and if we did notice we would not care—that Miss Havisham is a practical impossibility. No woman in this mortal world could possibly wear her wedding dress, leave untouched her marriage-reception table, for more than twenty years. That she could not, does not cross the mind of the "managed" reader. We are listening to a story of causes and intentions, and of their result in the Dickens World—not in our own everyday world. We know what Dickens means. He is bodying forth the unbearable grief of Miss Havisham abandoned by her betrothed on the morning of her marriage. It does not matter that her grief can have concrete results only in the world that Dickens creates, and not in ours.

Dickens, the conscious builder of plots, does not manage us nearly so well. We can, perhaps, believe that Magwitch would turn over all his money to Pip. With a greater effort, we agree to believe that Estella could, perhaps, be Magwitch's daughter. But when Orlick finds out about Magwitch, and lures Pip into a trap from which he is rescued at the last possible instant by his friend Herbert Pocket, who happened to find a note that seemed to contradict another note . . . we rebel. We are no longer being entertained. Dickens is not persuading us to believe the inconceivable. He is asking us to accept the impossible. We refuse.

There is a message in *Great Expectations*. It is there, as obvious and as unblushing as the message in the *Christmas Carol*. The story of Pip is the other half of the story of Scrooge. Scrooge had to learn how to be generous. Pip must learn how to receive. The money that Magwitch gives Pip nearly turns him not into a gentleman but a snob and a boor. Dickens was again building into a novel some of his ideas on the use and misuse of money.

Dickens the creator, though, is much more powerful than Dickens the moralist. After a year or two, we may have forgotten the very logical and reasonable steps that

Dickens had Pip follow in order to become a decent, upright man. But we have not forgotten the first time that Pip, when he is just a little boy, meets Magwitch in the graveyard:

"Hold your noise!" cried a terrible voice, as a man started up from among the graves at the side of the church . . . "Keep still, you little devil, or I'll cut your throat!"

A fearful man, all in coarse grey, with a great iron on his leg. A man with no hat, and with broken shoes, and with an old rag tied round his head. A man who had been soaked in water, and smothered in mud, and lamed by stones, and cut by flints, and stung by nettles, and torn by briars; who limped, and shivered, and glared and growled; and whose teeth chattered in his head as he seized me by the chin. . . .

"Tell us your name!" said the man. "Quick."

"Pip, sir."

"Once more," said the man, staring at me. "Give it mouth!"

"Pip. Pip, sir."

"Show us where you live," said the man. "Pint out the place!"

I pointed to where our village lay, on the flat inshore among the alder-trees and pollards, a mile or more from the church.

The man, after looking at me for a moment, turned me upside down, and emptied my pockets. There was nothing in them but a piece of bread. When the

church came to itself—for he was so sudden and
strong that he made it go head over heels before me,
and I saw the steeple under my feet—when the
church came to itself, I say, I was seated on a high
tombstone, trembling, while he ate the bread rave-
nously.

"You young dog," said the man, licking his lips,
"what fat cheeks you ha' got. . . ."

After darkly looking at his leg and at me several
times, he came closer to my tombstone, took me by
both arms, and tilted me back as far as he could hold
me; so that his eyes looked most powerfully down into
mine, and mine looked most helplessly up into his.

"Now lookee here," he said, "the question being
whether you're to be let to live. You know what a file
is?"

"Yes, sir."

"And you know what wittles is?"

"Yes, sir."

After each question he tilted me over a little more,
so as to give me a greater sense of helplessness and
danger.

"You get me a file." He tilted me again. "And you
get me wittles." He tilted me again. "You bring 'em
both to me." He tilted me again. "Or I'll have your
heart and liver out. . . ."

He gave me a most tremendous dip and roll, . . .
and went on in these fearful terms:

"You bring me, to-morrow morning early, that file
and them wittles. You bring the lot to me, at that old

Battery over yonder. You do it, and you never dare
to say a word or dare to make a sign concerning your
having seen such a person as me, or any person sum-
ever, and you shall be let to live. . . ."

In November, 1861, young Charley Dickens married.
His bride was Bessie Evans, the daughter of Frederick
Evans of Bradbury & Evans. Catherine had not gone to
Kate's wedding. Dickens did not go to Charley's. He had
not patched up his quarrel with Evans, and Charley's mar-
riage seemed to him a sort of betrayal of the family affec-
tions. However, he relented toward Charley before long.
He was soon a grandfather, and grandfatherly love over-
came hard feelings in a matter of business. Dickens and
Charley and Bessie and little Mary Angela ("Micketty")
Dickens spent the Christmas of 1862 together at Gad's Hill.

He did not relent with Phiz. Phiz—Hablôt Browne—
had for years done illustrations for Dickens's books, and
done them, it was widely felt, very well. He was a shy
man, and not a very sociable one. He and Dickens worked
together for years, but they did not become close friends.
When Bradbury & Evans founded *Once a Week*, after
Dickens had left *Household Words* and started *All the
Year Round*, Phiz decided to join its staff. Perhaps he dis-
approved of Dickens's noisy discussions of his troubles with
Catherine. In any case, Dickens thought that he had disap-
proved, and Phiz followed Bradbury, Evans, and Lemon
into the limbo of his dislike. Marcus Stone, Frank Stone's
son, became his illustrator.

Dickens was now nearly as famous as a public reader as

he was as a writer. In 1861 and 1862, he gave several series of readings in England and Scotland and in Paris. He was invited to make a reading tour of Australia. In six months there, a visiting Australian told him, he could earn £12,000 with his readings. Dickens seriously considered the idea, but in the end he decided not to go.

Perhaps, although he did not admit it, he felt that he was a little too old to make such a long, hard trip. When a man becomes a grandfather for the first time, he suddenly does feel that he may, perhaps, be growing a little old. When his friends and members of his own family die, the idea of age is brought home to him even more strongly. Not long after Dickens had rejected the idea of an Australian trip, he heard that Augustus Egg had died in Algiers. Then news came to him that his son Walter had died in Calcutta, at the age of twenty-two. "My poor boy was on his way home from an up-country station, on sick leave," Dickens wrote to Macready. "He had been very ill, but was not so at the time. He was talking to some brother officers in the Calcutta hospital about his preparations for home, when he suddenly became excited, had a rush of blood from the mouth, and was dead." And in September, 1863, Dickens's mother died.

On Christmas Eve of the same year, Thackeray died. Dickens and Thackeray had not been close friends. Their tastes and interests were too different. They had even quarreled hotly a number of times, and for several years after 1858, they had gone so far as to refuse to speak to each other. One day, in December, 1863, Thackeray met Dickens by chance. Bluntly, as was his way, Thackeray put out his hand. "It is time this foolish estrangement cease," he said. "Come: shake hands." They shook. Two weeks later, Thackeray was dead.

Dickens's own health was beginning to fail. This was a source of anguish to a man of his energy. He started a new novel—which he called *Our Mutual Friend*—early in 1864, but he found that he was writing more slowly than usual, and with greater difficulty. It was his left foot, in particular, that was causing him pain. He said that he had "got frostbitten by walking continually in the snow, and getting wet in the feet daily." Probably, he was, in fact, suffering from gout. But he would not give up his walks. He forced a shoe onto the aching foot every day, and set out. More than once, he returned home limping and in exquisite pain.

In May, 1865, he went to Paris for a short vacation. Ellen Ternan was with him. They recrossed the Channel from France back to England on June 9. Shortly after two o'clock in the afternoon, they were on their way to London on the Folkestone-to-London train.

At about quarter past three, the train was going along a straight stretch of track at fifty miles an hour. Unknown to the driver, a crew of workmen, who had misread a time-table and were not expecting a train along for another two hours, had ripped out the rails for repairs on a short bridge that crossed a stream. A safety man with a red flag was only five hundred yards from the stream. He ought to have been a thousand yards away. Anyway, it was too late. The driver put on all the brakes and threw the engine into reverse. When the train reached the stream, it was still going thirty miles an hour.

The engine itself leaped the stream and landed on the other bank. The baggage car and the second car were thrown over onto the next track. The third car, where Dickens and Ellen sat, was upended. The cars behind them plowed down the bank of the stream, overturned, and were smashed. A few cars at the end of the train stayed upright on the tracks.

Almost miraculously, Dickens and Ellen were unhurt. Dickens remained absolutely calm. He used his authoritative voice, which served him so well in his public readings, to help avert a panic. For several hours, he worked with the rescuers, who were freeing people trapped in the wreckage. He bathed wounds with water that he carried up from the stream in his hat, and gave sips of brandy to the injured and the dying, from a flask that he had in his pocket. When, finally, he had done as much as he could, he remembered that part of the manuscript of *Our Mutual Friend* was still in the car that he had been riding in, and he went back and got it.

As some people are, Dickens was calm in the crisis, and unnerved afterward. As a result of the accident, he did not feel entirely well until late in the month. It was the memory of the shrieks of the people that had been seriously hurt, and of the sight of the blood and the pain, that kept him "curiously weak—weak as if I were recovering from a long illness." For several years afterward, he dreaded train travel, and whenever a train that he was on clicked and rattled through a switch, beads of sweat would start out on his forehead.

Five years after that wreck, to the day, and nearly to the hour, Dickens died.

Our Mutual Friend was finished in September, 1865. It was Dickens's last complete novel. It has never been one of his more popular ones. Compared with most of his other works, *Our Mutual Friend* is slow and heavy. One might even say of it something that can rarely be said of anything that Dickens wrote: in places it is dull.

There are fine moments in the novel. The story of Bradley Headstone's love for Lizzie Hexam is powerfully told. Mr. Podsnap seems to sum up in one man, many of the things that Dickens particularly disliked: smugness, narrow-mindedness, pompousness, and false pride:

Mr. Podsnap was well to do, and stood very high in Mr. Podsnap's opinion. Beginning with a good inheritance, he had married a good inheritance, and had thriven exceedingly in the Marine Insurance way, and was quite satisfied. He never could make out why everybody was not quite satisfied, and he felt conscious that he set a brilliant social example in being particularly well satisfied with most things, and, above all other things, with himself.

Some people think that in Mr. Podsnap, Dickens was finally portraying John Forster, or portraying, at least, some of

the snobbish attitudes and bullying ways that Forster, for
some reason, adopted whenever he was in company:

In the meantime, a stray personage of a meek demeanour, who had wandered to the hearthrug and got
among the heads of tribes assembled there in confer-
ence with Mr. Podsnap, eliminated Mr. Podsnap's
flush and flourish by a highly unpolite remark; no
less than a reference to the circumstance that some
half-dozen people had lately died in the streets of starvation. It was clearly ill-timed, after dinner . . . It
was not in good taste. . . .

"I don't believe it," said Mr. Podsnap, putting it
behind him.

The meek man was afraid we must take it as
proved, because there were the Inquests and the Reg-
istrar's returns.

"Then it was their own fault," said Mr. Podsnap. . . .

The man of meek demeanour intimated that truly
it would seem from the facts as if starvation had been
forced upon the culprits in question—as if, in their
wretched manner, they had made their weak protests
against it—as if they would have taken the liberty of
staving it off if they could—as if they would rather
not have been starved upon the whole, if perfectly
agreeable to all parties.

"There is not," said Mr. Podsnap, flushing angrily,
"there is not a country in the world, sir, where so

noble a provision is made for the poor as in this country."

The meek man was quite willing to concede that,
but perhaps it rendered the matter even worse, as
showing that there must be something appallingly
wrong somewhere.

"Where?" said Mr. Podsnap.

The meek man hinted, Wouldn't it be well to try,
very seriously, to find out where?

"Ah!" said Mr. Podsnap. "Easy to say somewhere;
not so easy to say where! But I see what you are driving at. I knew it from the first. Centralization. No.
Never with my consent. Not English. . . ."

He was not aware (the meek man submitted of
himself) that he was driving at any ization. He had
no favourite ization that he knew of. But he certainly
was more staggered by these terrible occurrences than
he was by names, of howsoever so many syllables.
Might he ask, was dying of destitution and neglect
necessarily English? . . .

But Mr. Podsnap felt that the time had come for
flushing and flourishing this meek man down for
good. So he said:

"I must decline to pursue this painful discussion.
It is not pleasant to my feelings. It is repugnant to my
feelings. I have said that I do not admit these things.
I have also said that if they do occur (not that I admit
it), the fault lies with the sufferers themselves. It is
not for *me*"—Mr. Podsnap pointed "me" forcibly, as
adding by implication, though it may be all very well

for *you*—"it is not for me to impugn the workings of Providence. I know better than that, I trust . . . Besides," said Mr. Podsnap . . . "the subject is a very disagreeable one. I will go so far as to say it is an odious one. It is not one to be introduced among our wives and young persons, and I—" He finished with that flourish of his arm which added more expressively than any words: And I remove it from the face of the earth.

This is brilliant stuff; and *Our Mutual Friend* would be a brilliant novel if Dickens had managed to write it all at this level. Unfortunately, in other parts of the book, the pace lags. The old Dickensian fire burns a little low on many of the pages. We can almost see Dickens while he is writing, determined in spite of everything to go on "sweetening (and teaching) the fancies of others." We can almost see him between chapters, once more jamming his painful foot into a shoe, determined to take his ten-mile walk. He comes back from the walk, limping and weary. It was hard work. And it was hard work for him to write *Our Mutual Friend*. We sense it. Parts of it turn out to be not easy for us to read.

By January of 1866, Dickens's health was obviously getting worse. A doctor suggested to him that it might be heart trouble. In spite of this warning, and perhaps in order to try to get rid of his bad health by simply paying no attention to it, Dickens made arrangements to go on another reading tour. The firm of Messrs. Chappell undertook to make all the business arrangements connected with the tour, and they appointed a man named George Dolby to accompany Dickens as his manager.

This tour, which took Dickens from London to Glasgow and Edinburgh and back to Portsmouth, was a financial and personal success; but at the end of it, in May, he felt even worse than he had at the beginning of the year. He had difficulty in sleeping. He had a sharp pain in his left eye and a dull aching in his chest. Even so, he planned to force himself on. Chappell's proposed that he give another series of forty-two readings at the end of the year, from which he would earn £2,500. Dickens said something about hoping to be able to leave his family financially secure when he died, and agreed to do the readings. This second series started at Christmas and ended in May, 1867. In the course of it, Dickens went to Birmingham, Newcastle, and Liverpool, and across the Irish Sea to Belfast and Dublin. The constant traveling was plainly exhausting him. At night he was so worn out that he could hardly get undressed, and still it was hard for him to get to sleep.

Forster and Wills were dismayed when Dickens revealed to them, early in the summer, that he was thinking seriously of doing a series of readings in America. They used every possible argument that they could think of to dissuade him. Dickens merely answered that he was "drawn to America, as Charles Darnay had been drawn to the Lodestone Rock, Paris . . . ."

A farewell dinner was given for him on November 2, 1867. Five hundred people were present. At the end of the meal, Bulwer Lytton rose and made a few remarks paying tribute to Dickens's genius. When Dickens got up to speak, the storm of applause that greeted him was like nothing he had ever seen or heard before. All five hundred people in the room jumped to their feet, shouting and clapping their hands. Men tossed napkins, handkerchiefs, glasses into the air, and climbed up onto the chairs and the tables, where they roared and cheered some more. "God bless you, Mr. Dickens, for the light you have been in my house this many a year!"

Dickens tried to speak, but for once his voice failed him. As he gazed out over the banquet hall, at the sea of loving and beloved faces, tears came into his eyes, and he stood silent before the crowd and wept unashamed.

Dickens arrived in Boston on November 19, 1867. The city welcomed him with even greater warmth and enthusiasm than it had twenty-five years before. All the old grievances of the *American Notes* and *Chuzzlewit* seemed to have been forgotten. Pickwick snuff and Little Nell cigars were for sale throughout the city. Pictures of Dickens hung in hotel lobbies and restaurants and shopwindows. Men's stores did a brisk business in Dickens collars, which had a little likeness of Dickens on each tip. There was only this difference between the 1867 and the 1842 trips: the crowds did not mill after him now wherever he went, trying to shake his hand or to snip souvenirs from his thinning head of hair. The word had got about that he "wished to be quiet." He was even able to take a walk every day, and not be followed or talked to as he went.

He saw many of his old friends: Dr. Howe and Richard

Henry Dana, Jr., and Longfellow. His old secretary, George Putnam, came to call. He was "grey, and with several front teeth out, but I would have known him anywhere," Dickens wrote to Georgina.

The Boston readings were as great a triumph as any that he had ever done in England. John Greenleaf Whittier, the gentle old Quaker poet who had the year before written his famous *Snow-Bound*, summed up what everyone in the audience thought. "Those marvellous characters of his come forth," he wrote to the writer Celia Thaxter, ". . . as if their original creator had breathed new life into them. . . . Another such star-shower is not to be expected in one's lifetime."

The readings in New York were just as successful. Hundreds of people lined up all night outside Steinway Hall to get their tickets, despite the bitter December weather. Unfortunately, Dickens caught a cold, and the pain in his chest returned. A doctor was called. He urged Dickens to give up the readings altogether for a time. Dickens thanked him for the advice, but he did not take it. He lost his appetite. He slept badly. He did agree not to try to include Canada or the middle west of the United States in his tour. But he did not miss any of the scheduled readings because of his health.

From New York, he went south to Baltimore and on to Washington. President Andrew Johnson, most of the Cabinet, and all of the Supreme Court Justices attended his first reading, and rose to their feet applauding at the end of it. In Washington, he met Edwin M. Stanton, Secretary of War in Johnson's Cabinet. Stanton told him that at a Cabi-

Dickens on a reading tour

net meeting two years before, when Abraham Lincoln was still alive, a strange incident had taken place. Lincoln told the members of the Cabinet, before the meeting formally began, that he had had a bad dream the night before. It was, he thought, the third time in his life that he had had that same dream. "I am on a great, broad, rolling river," Lincoln said, "and I am in a boat—and I drift—and I drift —" He interrupted himself at that point and said, "But this is not business. Let us proceed to business, gentlemen." The day on which this Cabinet meeting had taken place was Good Friday, April 14, 1865. That night, at Ford's Theater in Washington, Lincoln was shot.

Not long after Dickens's meeting with Stanton, President Johnson dismissed Stanton from his post, without notifying the Senate. For this, and other moves, the President (of whom Dickens had formed the impression that he was "a man not to be turned or trifled with") was impeached, and the country went briefly into such a state of political excitement, that even attendance at the readings fell off. Dickens canceled a few, waiting for the crisis in Washington to die down, but early in March, he took up the tour again, in the upstate cities of New York. On March 20, he was back in New England. He was to go to New Haven, Hartford, New Bedford, and Portland, and then back to Boston and New York.

By the time that Dickens got to Portland, it was clear that he was very sick. He coughed for three or four hours every night. He no longer took his walks. He had all but lost his appetite and had begun to dose himself with laudanum, in the hope of being able to get some sleep at night.

In spite of the urging of friends and doctors, he insisted on doing every reading that had been set up. He read supremely well, but the toll on his health was terrible. As soon as he had finished a reading and gone offstage, he would fall onto a couch and lie there for several minutes, without speaking, breathless and bathed in sweat. He was now able to eat virtually no solid food at all. He lived on sherry with a raw egg in it, cream, strong beef tea, and champagne. But he would not give up. In part, it was his lifelong habit of punctuality and neatness that sent him out onto the stage night after night. In part, it was that he felt, within himself, that he owed the United States this much, by way of unspoken apology for his *American Notes*, and for the glib and bitter American chapters in *Chuzzlewit*. In part, he was almost hypnotically attracted by the storms of applause that greeted him on his every appearance.

By the middle of April, he was in New York. Only two more public duties were yet to be accomplished before he left for England. There was a public farewell banquet to attend, and a final reading to give. The day of the banquet, Dickens was so sick that he could hardly move. His foot and leg were swollen and painful. But he had the leg bandaged; and, one hour late, he limped into the banquet hall, his face twisted with pain. It was his duty, he felt, to be there. Twenty-five years before, he had, over and over again, insisted on speaking out about copyright laws and about slavery. Now he had one more thing to say; and, again, he insisted on saying it :

156

. . . how astounded I have been by the amazing
changes I have seen around me on every side—
changes moral, changes physical, changes in the
amount of land subdued and peopled, changes in the
rise of vast new cities, changes in the growth of older
cities almost out of recognition, changes in the graces
and amenities of life, changes in the press . . . Nor
am I, believe me, so arrogant as to suppose that in
twenty-five years there have been no changes in me,
and that I had nothing to learn, and no extreme im-
pressions to correct when I was here first . . . In the
smallest places, equally with the largest, I have been
received with unsurpassable politeness, delicacy,
sweet-temper, hospitality, consideration, and with unsurpassable respect for the privacy daily enforced
upon me by the nature of my avocation here, and the
state of my health. This testimony, so long as I live,
and so long as my descendants have any legal right
in my books, I shall cause to be re-published as an ap-
pendix to those two books of mine in which I have
referred to America.

On April 22, Dickens was to sail for home. He came out
of his hotel to find an enormous crowd assembled in the
street to bid him good-bye. From the windows of the buildings nearby, a rain of flowers fell on him. When he got into
his carriage, a tremendous cheer went up: "Good-bye!
Good-bye, Boz!" And on the deck of his ship, the cry of
their respect and their love reached his ears. "Good-bye,

Boz! God bless you." Dickens, sick and tired, his leg in terrible pain, put his hat on his walking stick and waved it in the air, as Tiny Tim had waved his crutch. He called back to the crowd what Tiny Tim had said: "God bless us, every one!"

CHAPTER 12

"The Footsteps Die Out"

On his second trip, Dickens had spent one hundred and fifty-five days in America. During that time he had traveled, with few pauses and little rest, more than five thousand miles. He had given seventy-six readings, which is to say that he had given a reading, practically speaking, every two days. Each of the readings was an acting performance of a high order. Dickens put into each one every bit of mental and physical energy that he could muster. He had lived for four months in a state of rapidly alternating tension and exhaustion. When he got back to England in May, 1868, his health was shattered.

If he had taken a long rest, all might yet have been well. But he would not, or could not. Wills had had an accident while Dickens was away, and had been obliged to resign from *All the Year Round*. Dickens took over, for a time, many of Wills's duties on the magazine. A play called *No Thoroughfare*, which Dickens and Wilkie Collins had written in collaboration, had been translated into French and was about to be put on in Paris. A few weeks after he had returned home, Dickens went to Paris to supervise the final rehearsals. Young Charley Dickens had been taken onto the staff of *All the Year Round*, and was doing good work. Dickens was able to shift some of his burden onto the shoulders of his son. Even so, his health grew worse rather than better. During the summer, he admitted to Forster that he was unable to make out the words on the left-hand side of such things as signs over the doors of shops.

Yet he planned to start another series of readings, early in October. While he was still in America, he had signed an agreement with Chappell's that he would do one hundred readings for £8,000—or today about $120,000. Over the summer, he prepared and rehearsed a new passage to put into his programs. He took it from *Oliver Twist*. It was about the murder of Nancy, and the flight and death of Sikes. Like all of his readings, it was to be done with gestures and with a different voice for each of the characters; and when Nancy was being killed, Dickens gave forth terrifying reproductions of her pleas for mercy, and her dying screams:

The girl was lying half-dressed upon [the bed.] He had roused her from her sleep, for she raised herself with a hurried and startled look.

"Get up!" said the man.

"It *is* you, Bill!" said the girl, with an expression of pleasure at his return.

"It is," was the reply. "Get up."

There was a candle burning, but the man hastily

drew it from the candlestick, and hurled it under the grate. Seeing the faint light of early day without, the girl rose to undraw the curtain.

"Let it be," said Sikes, thrusting his hand before her. "There's light enough for wot I've got to do."

"Bill," said the girl, in a low voice of alarm, "why do you look like that at me?"

The robber sat regarding her, for a few seconds, with dilated nostrils and heaving breast; and then, grasping her by the head and throat, dragged her into the middle of the room, and looking once towards the door, placed his heavy hand upon her mouth.

"Bill, Bill!" gasped the girl, wrestling with the strength of mortal fear—"I—I won't scream or cry —not once—hear me—speak to me—tell me what I have done!"

"You know, you she-devil!" returned the robber, suppressing his breath. "You were watched to-night; every word you said was heard."

"Then spare my life for the love of Heaven, as I spared yours," rejoined the girl, clinging to him. "Bill, dear Bill, you cannot have the heart to kill me. . . ."

The housebreaker freed one arm, and grasped his pistol. The certainty of immediate detection if he fired flashed across his mind even in the midst of his fury; and he beat it twice, with all the force he could summon, upon the upturned face that almost touched his own.

161

She staggered and fell, nearly blinded with the blood that rained down from a deep gash in her fore-head. . . .

The murderer, staggering backwards to the wall, and shutting out the sight with his hand, seized a heavy club and struck her down.

Forster, George Dolby, young Charley, and a number of others heard this reading before Dickens did it in public. They all tried to persuade him to leave it off his program. They argued that it was so bloodcurdling a performance that the audiences might become hysterical. What they really feared was that because the murder required so much effort and energy, Dickens might, one evening, die on stage, right while he was reading it.

Dickens, as usual, had his own way. He read the murder of Nancy in public first in London, on January 5, 1869. The audience was white-faced and terror-stricken at the end of it. The evening was a triumphant success. Dickens himself was, for twelve hours afterward, in a state of near-collapse. He insisted, however, on forcing himself through the tour, and on reading Nancy and Sikes three evenings out of every four.

He crossed to Ireland in the middle of January. On the trip from Belfast to Dun Laoghaire, he was involved in another, but a less serious, train accident. Back in England, he read in the town of Cheltenham, where Macready, seventy-six years old and very sick and weak, came to hear him. At Clifton, when Dickens read the murder, about

Charles Dickens, 1868, two years before his death

twenty ladies in the audience fainted and had to be carried out of the hall.

By the middle of April, his left leg was lame, and his left hand and arm were all but paralyzed. It became obvious even to him that he could not go on. He had done seventy-four of the scheduled one hundred readings. A London doctor named Sir Thomas Watson persuaded him to cancel the others. Dickens sadly agreed. He agreed, that is, to do no more readings for six months at least, and then to do only twelve final ones, and those in London. He must do those twelve, he said. Otherwise he would be dealing most unfairly with Chappell's.

In July, Dickens started work on a new novel: *The Mystery of Edwin Drood*. He was able to write only half of it before he died.

Edwin Drood is engaged to Rosa Budd. Edwin's uncle, John Jasper, an opium addict, is also in love with Rosa, but she feels only loathing for him. Edwin finally decides that neither Rosa's nor his own happiness could result from their marrying, and he breaks off the engagement, but without telling John Jasper. A young man named Neville Landless has several times reproved Edwin for his cool behavior toward Rosa. Both Edwin and Neville have dinner with Jasper on Christmas Eve. On Christmas Day, Edwin is missing. Neville is tried, but since Edwin's body cannot be found, the case is dismissed. Jasper swears that he will destroy the murderer of "the dear dead boy." Then Jasper himself is put under observation by a Mr. Datchery. Because of his head of flowing white hair and his dark black eyebrows, Mr. Datchery gives the impression of being someone, either a man or a woman, in disguise . . .

This is as far as Dickens got. He left no notes, no sketches of a plot outline, to show how he had intended to finish the story.

True to his word to himself and to Chappell's, Dickens began a series of twelve readings on January 11, 1870.

His foot was causing him great pain. A doctor went to every reading and insisted that young Charley go to them all as well: "You must be there every night, and if you see your father falter in the least, you must run and catch him and bring him off to me, or, by Heaven, he'll die before them all."

Dickens would not hear of eliminating the murder of Nancy from the program, even though the reading of it caused his pulse to rise from 72 to 112. During the intermission, he would lie speechless and exhausted on a sofa backstage; but after ten or fifteen minutes, he would miraculously pull himself together, and go back on stage to finish the program. The audiences had heard it said that he was not in good health, but he was so able an actor that he gave no sign before the public of how seriously sick he was. He read, as always, brilliantly well. Only on the last three evenings did his illness interfere at all with his performance, and even then, very few people noticed it: several times he said "Pickswick" or "Picnic" instead of "Pickwick."

On the final evening, March 15, 1870, there were two thousand people present to hear him, including little Micketty Dickens. At the end of the last reading, there came a tumult of cheering. He had finished in triumph. He knew that he would have no more chances to see the beloved crowds, the masses of people for whose pleasure and delight he had always worked so hard. He returned to the stage for a moment, and spoke: "From these garish lights I now vanish forevermore with a heartfelt, grateful, respectful, affectionate farewell."

He could sleep now only if he took laudanum. His foot, he said, was "a bag of pain." There were deep lines in his face, and his hair was nearly white. He still took long walks; but he went very slowly, and he limped badly.

Even so, he kept up his incessant activity. He had a private audience with Queen Victoria at Buckingham Palace. He had breakfast with William Gladstone, who was then Prime Minister. He had dinner several days later with Benjamin Disraeli, who was to become Prime Minister in four years. He went to a dinner given in honor of the King of Belgium. In May, he once again directed a company of amateur actors. He had even hoped to be able to do a part in the play himself, but the pain in his leg and foot prevented him. On May 22, he saw Forster for the last time.

On June 8, neither Mary nor Kate was at Gad's Hill. Dickens spent the day at work on *Edwin Drood*. He and Georgina sat down to dinner punctually at six o'clock. Georgina saw that his face was contracted with pain. Dickens said that, for the past hour or so, he had been feeling very ill. All the same, he did want to have dinner.

Suddenly, he said to Georgina that he must go to London right away. He pushed back his chair and stood up. In alarm, Georgina rose and rushed around the table to where he was. If she had not caught him, he would have fallen to the floor. As it was, he weighed too much for her, and he gradually sank down through her arms onto his left side on the carpet. In a faint voice, he murmured the last words that he was to speak. "Yes—on the ground. . . ."

Georgina, with the help of the servants, lifted him and put him on the sofa that was in the dining room. He did not stir or give any sign. Georgina at once summoned the local doctor, and sent telegrams to Mary and Kate and Charley. Mary and Kate arrived six hours later. Charley got there early the next morning, and a doctor from London came with him.

Dickens lay unconscious on the sofa all through the night and the next day. Kate hurried back to London to tell Catherine what had happened. In the afternoon, Ellen Ternan arrived. Dickens was breathing regularly and heavily, but he gave no other sign of life.

At a few minutes after six in the evening, he sighed deeply. A tear formed in his right eye, welled out, glistened for an instant on his cheek, and was gone. Charles Dickens was dead.

They buried him in Westminster Abbey at six o'clock in the morning, June 14. He had asked that his funeral be quiet and private. Only four of his children were in England. They were at the funeral, and Georgina and Forster and Wilkie Collins and only a very few others.

His grave was not finally closed for three days. During that time, an unending procession of people filed by his coffin. Great mounds of flowers heaped up around him. At midnight on June 16, 1870, the tomb was sealed.

Chronology

1812   Charles Dickens born, Landport, England, February 7.

1823   Becomes potboy in blacking factory.

1827   Finishes school; becomes shorthand reporter in Doctors' Commons court.

1830   Falls in love with Maria Beadnell.

1832   Becomes newspaper and journal reporter.

1833   Has first manuscript accepted, by *Monthly Magazine*.

1836   First installment of *Pickwick Papers* on sale, March 31; marries Catherine Hogarth, April 2.

1837   Publishes *Oliver Twist*, February; Sister-in-law, Mary, dies, May.

1838   Publishes *Nicholas Nickleby*.

1841   Publishes *The Old Curiosity Shop* and *Barnaby Rudge;* receives freedom of city of Edinburgh, June 25.

169

1842   Dickens and wife sail for America, January 4; Tours country for six months. Writes *American Notes*.

1843   Publishes *A Christmas Carol* and *Martin Chuzzlewit*.

1844   Travels to Italy with family for one year.

1846   Publishes *Dombey and Son*.

1849   Publishes *David Copperfield*.

1850   John Dickens, Charles's father, dies.

1853   Publishes *Bleak House;* gives first public reading, December.

1854   Publishes *Hard Times*.

1857   Publishes *Little Dorrit*.

1858   Is separated from his wife. Tours England, Scotland, Ireland, giving public readings.

1859   Publishes *A Tale of Two Cities*.

1860   Publishes *Great Expectations*.

1865   Is involved in train wreck.

1866   Undertakes second reading tour.

1867   Travels to America for second time, November.

1870   Charles Dickens dies, June 8.

The Major Novels of Dickens

Listed below, in alphabetical order, are the novels generally considered today to be Dickens's major works. In parenthesis after the name of each title is the year of first publication; and since much of what Dickens wrote was published in serial form (a serial that was started in one year not infrequently continued into the next year), often two dates are given; for example, *Pickwick Papers* (1836–1837) —they are the two years in which the installments appeared. A very short summary of each work is also given. The list following each summary gives the names of some of the more memorable characters in the book.

Barnaby Rudge (1841)

A historical novel set in England at the end of the eighteenth century. The most famous pages are those that deal with the "Gordon" riots of 1780. Dolly Varden, Miggs.

Bleak House (1852–1853)

A novel based on the theme that lawyers and courts of justice too often act slowly and with grave incompetence.

Two plots are intertwined : one concerns Richard Carstone and Ada Clare and the fortune that they might inherit; the other concerns, chiefly, Lady Dedlock, her crime, and her payment for it. Jo, Mr. Vholes, Mr. Tulkinghorn, Mr. Chadband, Mrs. Jellyby, Miss Flite.

A Christmas Carol (1843)
The stingy Scrooge is reformed by a ghost, and behaves ever afterward with exemplary generosity to his poor clerk, Bob Cratchit. Ebenezer Scrooge, Bob Cratchit, Tiny Tim.

David Copperfield (1849–1850)
Dickens's autobiography, thinly veiled. Like Dickens, David, after a difficult childhood, becomes a famous writer. David, Mr. and Mrs. Micawber, Mr. and Miss Murdstone, Aunt Betsey Trotwood, Dora Spenlow Copperfield, Steerforth, Barkis, Peggotty, Uriah Heep, Mrs. Gummidge.

Dombey and Son (1846–1848)
The "decline and fall" of a cold, rich, proud, and insensitive nineteenth-century English businessman. Mr. Dombey, Paul Dombey, Carker, Toots, Major Bagstock.

Great Expectations (1860–1861)
A semi-autobiographical novel that deals with the fortunes and the misfortunes, the rise and the civilization of Pip—who, in many ways, is Dickens himself. Pip, Joe Gargery, Miss Havisham, Estella, Mr. Wemmick, Mr. Wemmick's Aged Parent.

172

Hard Times (1854)

One of Dickens's shortest novels. It considers several of the possible evil effects of the Industrial Revolution on persons and on events in a small English city. Mr. Gradgrind, Mr. Bounderby, Slackbridge, Mrs. Sparsit.

Little Dorrit (1857–1858)

A story of riches and poverty and debtors' prison, of family devotion and of snobbery. Amy Dorrit (Little Dorrit), Mr. Merdle, Flora Finching, Mr. Pancks, Mr. Casby.

Martin Chuzzlewit (1843–1844)

A novel that is about selfishness and hypocrisy, but that is often extremely funny. Some of the events in the story take place in the United States. Mr. Pecksniff, Cherry and Merry, Sairey Gamp, Betsy Prig, Mrs. Harris.

The Mystery of Edwin Drood (1870)

An unfinished "mystery" novel. John Jasper, Mr. Datchery, Mr. Sapsea.

Nicholas Nickleby (1838–1839)

Generosity and charity are contrasted with cruelty on the one hand, and empty-headedness on the other. The novel contains an attack on ill-run boarding schools. Mrs. Nickleby, Mr. Mantalini, Smike, Vincent Crummles, Newman Noggs.

173

The Old Curiosity Shop (1841)

The life, wanderings, and death of Little Nell Trent and her unfortunate grandfather. Nell and grandfather, Sampson Brass, Sally Brass, Kit, Dick Swiveller, Codlin and Short, The Marchioness.

Oliver Twist (1837–1838)

The life and adventures of Oliver, a boy who was born, of uncertain parentage, in a workhouse. The novel is Dickens's first direct attack on the evils of society. Oliver, Bumble, Mr. Sowerberry, Noah Claypole, Fagin, Charley Bates, The Artful Dodger, Nancy, Bill Sikes.

Our Mutual Friend (1864–1865)

Snobbery, self-satisfaction, attempted murder, and a love story. Eugene Wrayburn, Lizzie Hexam, Bradley Headstone, Mr. Podsnap.

Pickwick Papers (1836–1837)

Dickens's first major work. It is not, properly speaking, a novel but rather a loosely connected series of anecdotes and adventures. The principal incidents in the book are perhaps those that grow out of an unfortunate conversation that Mr. Pickwick holds with Mrs. Bardell. *Pickwick Papers* is said by many to be Dickens's liveliest and funniest book. Mr. Pickwick, Mr. Winkle, Mr. Tupman, Mr. Snodgrass, Sam Weller, Sam Weller's father, Jingle, Job Trotter, Mrs. Bardell, Serjeant Buzfuz, Pott.

Sketches by Boz (1836–1837)

These early, short pieces, some of them essays and descriptions, some of them fiction, were published in one volume in 1839. Mr. Minns, Mrs. Tiggs, The Tuggeses.

A Tale of Two Cities (1859)

A novel about the French Revolution, some of its causes and some of its effects. Jarvis Lorry, Jerry Cruncher, M. and Mme Defarge, Sydney Carton.

Books for Further Reading

Chesterton, G. K. *Charles Dickens*, 16th edition. London: Methuen, 1927.

Fielding, K. J. *Charles Dickens*, 2nd edition (enlarged). London: Longmans, 1965.

Ford, George H. *Dickens and His Readers*. Princeton: Princeton University Press, 1955 (and reprinted).

Forster, John. *The Life of Charles Dickens*. Edited by J. W. T. Ley. London: Cecil Palmer, 1928.

Gissing, George. *Critical Studies of the Works of Dickens*. New York: Haskell House, 1965 (reprinted).

Gross, John J. and Gabriel Pearson, editors. *Dickens and the Twentieth Century*. Toronto: University of Toronto Press, 1962.

House, Humphrey. *The Dickens World*. London: Oxford University Press, 1941 (several times reprinted).

Johnson, Edgar. *Charles Dickens: His Tragedy and Triumph*. Boston: Little, Brown, 1952.

Lindsay, Jack. *Charles Dickens*. London: Dakers, 1950.

Lane, Lauriat, Jr., and George H. Ford, editors. *The Dickens Critics*. Ithaca: Cornell University Press, 1961.

Marcus, Steven. *Dickens: from Pickwick to Dombey*. London: Chatto & Windus, 1965.

Pearson, Hesketh. *Dickens*. London: Methuen, 1949 (reprinted).

Pope-Hennessy, Una. *Charles Dickens*. New York: Howell, Soskin, 1946.

Wagenknecht, Edward. *The Man Charles Dickens*, revised edition. Norman: University of Oklahoma Press, 1966.

Index

INDEX